SOBERING TRADEMARK STORIES

COSTLY MISTAKES TO AVOID

BY DAVID L. HOFFMAN, ESQ.

WWW.DLHPATENT.COM
WWW.SOBERINGTRADEMARKSTORIES.COM

First soft cover edition June 2017

For information about special discounts for bulk purchases, please contact David L. Hoffman at (661) 775-0300 or david@DHLpatent.com

Interior design by C. Spencer Reynolds (www.SpencerReynolds.com)
Book cover design and layout by Ellie Bockert Augsburger of Creative Digital Studios. (www.CreativeDigitalStudios.com)

Cover design features:
Celebration: © Dmitriy Raykin / Adobe Stock
Scales: © Valdis Torms / Adobe Stock
Elegant Girl: © Denis Aglichev / Adobe Stock
Fashionable: © Andrey Kiselev/ Adobe Stock

ISBN-10: 0-9990891-0-2
ISBN-13: 978-0-9990891-0-1
Ebook ISBN: 978-0-9990891-1-8

ACKNOWLEDGEMENTS

This book was inspired by two things: my passion for every business to understand and protect their trademarks and all the wine tasting trips my wife and I have made. I would like to acknowledge my business coach and mentor Ken Keller of Strategic Advisory Boards™ for pushing me to write this book. Thanks also to Pat Kramer, Writer for Hire®, whose professional editing skills and suggestions greatly improved this work. And thanks to my friend Jennifer Brown for her final review of this book.

This book was also a family effort. My daughter Payton contributed the artwork on the back cover. My other daughter Ashton helped with editing and with clever chapter titles. Finally, thanks to my wife Christy for her non-stop support, excellent suggestions, and *never* saying, "Are you going to finish this thing or what?"

TABLE OF CONTENTS

INTRODUCTION:
Some Basic Trademark Law Principles

Trademarks go back to ancient times: Stone cutters would leave their mark in Egyptian structures as early as about 4,000 B.C.

Trademark laws, however, are much more recent. In England in 1862, the Merchandise Marks Act made it a criminal offense to copy another's trademark "with intent to defraud or to enable another to defraud." This provided some protection for trademark owners.

Right on the heels of England's initiation of trademark laws, in 1870 the U.S. enacted its own trademark laws. Congress believed it had the right to do so under the U.S. Constitution's copyright clause powers, but was confused by the differences between trademark and copyright law. Though the 1870 Act was struck down as unconstitutional, in 1881 Congress tried again and this time was successful, relying on the Commerce Clause powers.

Historically, producers of alcoholic beverages have always found it important to protect their marks. The very first registered mark in England was a red triangle for ale belonging to Bass Brewery, dating back to the 1600s.

The alcohol industry has some very longstanding trademarks. While the Bass Brewery claims use since the 1600s, Lowenbrau's claim for use goes back to 1383, and Stella Artois' is even older: 1366. The earliest record is from the German beer, Weihenstephaner, whose claim of use dates back to 1040, when the brand began as a way to inform buyers where its beer was made.

Likewise, wineries have similar claims for use. The world's oldest existing winery, the Groot Constantia vineyard and winery in South Africa, claims use since 1685, while the oldest existing winery in America appears to be Brotherhood Winery in the Hudson Valley town of Washingtonville, New York, which claims use since 1839.

Brotherhood Winery as seen in 1910

The history of trademarks and trademark laws raises some important concepts. For the nonexpert, understanding key differences between trademark and copyright protection is not easy. Even Congress got it wrong!

Simply put, copyright is about protecting artists' and writers' works (goods or services are irrelevant to that). Trademarks are about protecting the public from confusion over competing goods or services that are using the same or similar designations. For example, if you love Coke® or Pepsi®, the trademark helps ensure that if you order that brand, you will not get some other cola.

Trademarks are meant to protect consumers who are buying goods or services. Accordingly, trademark rights come from two things combined: (I) the mark, *and* (II) the goods or services for which the mark is used.

In addition, it is important to recognize the difference between the "right to register" a trademark and the "right to use" a trademark.

Registration of a mark helps trademark owners give notice of their rights and of their intent to enforce those rights. Whether or not a trademark may be allowed by the U.S. Trademark Office requires that the trademark be different enough (no "likelihood of confusion") from already existing trademark registrations and applications. Later on, we'll discuss specific examples that will help clarify what the "likelihood of confusion" standard means.

A trademark registration is like erecting a fence around your property. The fence will tell others that there is a property line and where that line is. However, just as you don't have to build a fence when you own property, you don't necessarily have to register a trademark to receive protection of your trademark rights: Trademark rights are established in a geographic area based on usage of the mark. However, it is still very important to register your trademark so that others are aware of your mark, should you need to enforce your rights.

Not only is it important to register your mark, but it's also very important to select a mark that does not infringe on someone else's trademark rights (or is so close to the line that the other trademark owner thinks it is infringing).

This book tells the stories of business owners who have run into trouble and either have been sued or have sued someone else. By showcasing these examples, I hope to help you avoid or mitigate trademark problems. As you read, feel free to use the glossary in the back of this book if there is a word or acronym that is unfamiliar to you.

Additionally, be sure to review the Conclusion and Appendix included at the end: Ten Tips to Protect Your Intellectual Property and a Checklist and Intellectual Property Self-Assessment. These two resources will help cement your understanding of trademarks and the law and help you be better prepared, should there be a challenge to your own trademark rights.

As always, please bear in mind that this book is not intended as legal advice or for reliance upon its research; it is for education and entertainment. If you need legal advice, be sure to consult an attorney who practices and is experienced in Trademark and Intellectual Property Law.

CHAPTER 1

TRADEMARKS AND SURNAMES: WHEN MAY A BUSINESS USE THE OWNER'S FAMILY NAME?

Many business owners believe that it is their right to use a family name for their business or product. Wineries and vineyard owners often use a family name in their business name, otherwise known as their "trade name." This becomes an issue when your family name is already in use by another business of the same name.

The law tries to allow a business owner to use his or her family name, as long as there is no confusion. Consider the family name "Gallo." If your last name were Gallo, could you open a vineyard or winery with that name? The answer is no. Why? Because the law of trademarks is meant to protect consumers, not businesses, and when you have a famous or well-known mark such as "Gallo," consumers will very likely be confused by another company's use of that same name.

Can Gallo family members use the name "Gallo" as a business name or trademark? No again–not without a license from Gallo. Even the brother of Ernest and Julio Gallo could not sell cheese under the name "Gallo" without a license from E. & J. Gallo Winery. So how can you know when you can safely use your family name?

If you are not dealing with a famous name, you stand at least some chance of being able to use your family name–providing you take pains to avoid confusing customers. This is a tricky matter and may take you into dangerous territory, as shown in the case of *E. & J. Gallo Winery v. Gallo Cattle Company*, 967 F.2d 1280 (9th Cir. 1992).

In the early 1900s, Joseph Gallo, Sr. and Assunto Bianco arrived in Northern California from Italy, marrying and having children shortly afterward. Ernest was born in 1909, Julio in 1910, and Joseph Jr. in 1919.

Joseph Sr. and Assunto ran saloons, bought grapes and made wine until Prohibition began in 1919. Then, they bought vineyards and grew grapes to sell to home winemakers in the East and Midwest. In 1932, after the Great Depression hit, Joseph Sr. killed his wife and then himself, possibly in despair over financial loses.

The following year, 1933, brothers Ernest and Julio founded the E. & J. Gallo Winery in Modesto, California, where they continued to make wine during prohibition for "medicinal use." The day Prohibition ended, E. & J. Gallo Winery shipped wine under the family name and trademark GALLO. When Joseph Jr. reached adulthood, he sued his older brothers for mishandling the proceeds of his stock in the winery. They entered into an agreement with Joseph Jr., paying him $20,000 and keeping the winery.

E. & J. Gallo Winery

Initially, Joseph worked for his brothers, purportedly turning down an oral offer of partnership in the winery. In 1955, Joseph opened a cattle farm called "Gallo Cattle Company." He also had a vineyard under the name "Joseph Gallo Vineyards." Ernest and Julio apparently did not complain about that.

In 1983, Joseph started selling cheese, wholesale, under the name "Gallo Cattle Company." The following year, Joseph entered the retail market using his name, JOSEPH GALLO,

as a trademark. E. & J. Gallo Winery's licensee, Gallo Salame, complained because they were already selling cheese (and salami) on a retail level. In 1986, E. & J. sued Joseph, his son Michael and the Gallo Cattle Company for trademark infringement.

The Trial Court ruled that there was infringement and issued an injunction directing Joseph, Michael and the Gallo Cattle Company not to sell cheese in the retail market using a mark having "Gallo" in it.

The United States Court of Appeals for the Ninth Circuit[1] upheld the injunction and explained that courts are reluctant to stop the use of a personal name as the name of one's business, as long as that use is not intended to confuse consumers. *E. & J. Gallo Winery v. Gallo Cattle Co.*, 967 F. 2d 1280 (9th Cir. 1992).

The Appeals Court believed that Joseph's use was intended to capitalize on the family name "Gallo" with people who buy cheese. However, the Court did not stop Joseph's other uses of Gallo. Thereafter, Joseph renamed the business JOSEPH FARMS, and that name is still being used to this day. According to Joseph's son Michael, Joseph took these legal battles very hard. He suffered strokes, and he stopped talking to his brothers.

1 The Ninth Circuit covers Alaska, Arizona, California, Hawaii, Idaho, Montana, Nevada, Oregon and Washington state, as well as Guam and the Northern Mariana Islands.

Lesson Learned: You are *not entitled* to use your own name as a trademark, if it is likely that it would cause confusion with an already existing trademark. However, even if you cannot use your own name as a trademark, you can use it on the label or in connection with the product or service being sold, as long as it is done in a truthful and nonconfusing way.

Bear in mind that where there are existing trademark rights in the desired name, you should be very careful. A disclaimer[2] does not always cure the issue, especially if your last name happens to be Gallo.

2 A "disclaimer" is where one business uses a notice that it has no affiliation with another business (or another business's product or service), e.g., "Gallo Cattle Company is not affiliated with E. & J. Gallo Winery."

CHAPTER 2

DUKING IT OUT: JOHN WAYNE'S HEIRS TAKE ON DUKE UNIVERSITY

"It's my name and I can use it" is a popular sentiment for naming a business or a product, but as demonstrated in the previous example, it is not always that simple. Many will remember John Wayne, also known as "The Duke" or "Duke." He was always tough and fearless. The Duke was an international icon and a beloved movie star.

There is another internationally known "Duke"–Duke University, often referred to as just "Duke." We can readily tell the difference, based on context, between the two "Dukes." Sadly, it is not so straightforward in the trademark world, as in the case of *John Wayne Enterprises, LLC v. Duke University et al*, Case No. 8:14-cv-01020 (C.D.Ca. 2017).

John Wayne was born in 1907 and moved to the Los Angeles area with his family when he was a young boy. He had a dog named "Duke," and that also became Wayne's nickname. The Duke went to USC on a football scholarship but while bodysurfing, he broke his collar bone, ending his athletic aspirations. It was then that he set his sights on becoming a movie star.

The Duke's first role was as a stand-in for a football player, and in 1930, he got his first leading role in the movie *The Big Trail*. Although he was cast in many "B" movies, his career blossomed in 1939 after he had a leading role in *Stagecoach*. Over the course of 40 years, he starred in 142 pictures and earned multiple Academy Award nominations.

The Duke battled cancer and survived until 1979 when he succumbed to stomach cancer at the age of 72. His last wish was that his fame be used to support the fight against cancer. To that end, The Duke's heirs created John Wayne Enterprises (JWE) which has commercialized The Duke's name, nickname and likeness. Its products have included T-shirts, artwork, knives, hats, leather goods, glassware and spirits, among other things.

JWE is no stranger to trademark applications. It has filed approximately 70 federal applications. The earliest one it filed on DUKE was for firearms, in 1982. In 2003, it filed on DUKE for clothing, which was pending for about eight years, then abandoned due to other registrations and/or applications having DUKE therein. To get DUKE registered for bourbon, JWE undoubtedly knew it had to avoid rejection over several other registrations on DUKE or variations of it, some of which were owned by Duke University.

In early 2013, JWE decided to name its bourbon "DUKE" and filed an intent to use[3] (ITU) trademark application for "alcoholic beverages except beers." JWE later distilled and bottled the bourbon through a deal with Monument Valley Distillers.

To help distinguish over other marks using DUKE, JWE listed the goods as "[a]lcoholic beverages except beers, all in connection with indicia denoting the late internationally-known movie star John Wayne, who is also known as Duke."

Duke University, also familiar with federal trademark applications, has filed approximately 120 of them. This

3 An "intent to use" (ITU) trademark application is generally one where the trademark owner (applicant) has not yet "used" the mark (or is not sure of "use"), but does have a "good faith" intent to use the mark. "Use" in a trademark sense comes from actual sales of the goods with the trademark on the goods or their packaging, or actual sales of the services with the trademark used in advertisements for its services.

venerable educational institution has many registrations using DUKE for various apparel. The University, like JWE, also has had troubles with trademarks on DUKE. It took about eleven years to get DUKE for apparel registered.

The First Opposition Proceeding

The Trademark Office did not have an issue with JWE's application on DUKE for "alcoholic beverages." However, after the Trademark Office published the application indicating its intention to register the mark, Duke University filed an opposition to the registration. The University listed many trademark registrations, none of which mentioned use of DUKE in relation to any alcohol.

The Second and Third Oppositions

JWE also filed applications on DUKE 44-40 and DUKE JOHN WAYNE with the same or similar alcohol goods as in its DUKE application. The Trademark Office would have allowed these applications as well, but Duke University opposed them too.

Duke University, like "Duke" John Wayne, is also a household name. Its beginnings go back to 1838 as "Brown's Schoolhouse." It underwent some further name changes. Then it moved to Durham, North Carolina, before the turn of the century, with the benefit of a generous donation by Washington Duke, a tobacco magnate. The school, then Trinity College, became Duke University in 1924 after Washington Duke's son provided a $40 million endowment.

Although the school was founded by Methodists and Quakers, ironically the mascot and nickname became the "Blue Devils." Duke's blue color is very well known, especially to college basketball fans. The Blue Devils have been among the final four teams at the annual NCAA basketball tournament 16 times, and won the tournament five times. Duke has also been ranked in the Top 10 schools for academics.

The University Store at Duke sells a wide variety of DUKE branded goods, such as clothing, glassware, bags, sports equipment and books; there is even a DUKE lamp with a blue lampshade. Duke University also has an extensive trademark licensing program. Like any major institution, Duke protects its trademarks.

The JWE Lawsuit for Noninfringement

An opposition in the Trademark Office is a lot like litigation. However, many oppositions settle very quickly. In this case, JWE decided to try to bypass the Trademark Office proceedings by filing suit in federal court in California for a declaration that JWE's DUKE mark on bourbon does not infringe Duke University's trademarks.

In response, Duke University moved to dismiss the lawsuit arguing that California is not the right place for it. In September 2014, the Court agreed and dismissed the suit.

Duke University Files a Fourth Opposition

The fight in the Trademark Office still raged on. Now it involved four JWE applications, because Duke University also opposed JWE's DINING WITH THE DUKE for magazines and online magazines about food and alcohol. Ultimately, JWE amended the description of its mark and the services in this DINING WITH THE DUKE application to indicate that the mark would not be in the color blue and the magazines would be marketed in a manner to associate the term DUKE with John Wayne. After that amendment, the oppositions were dismissed.

This battle points out a very important difference between fighting in court and fighting in the Trademark Office. In the Trademark Office, it does not matter what JWE's actual bottle label is. The Trademark Office only looks at the mark that the application is on.

The *actual label* for JWE's *bourbon* has a picture of John Wayne on it, his signature and a star. (See below left). The JWE *application* for alcohol was on the mark DUKE in typed form (see below right), which is significantly more likely to be confused with Duke University's marks than the actual label.

JWE "DUKE" BOURBON
ACTUAL LABEL

DUKE

JWE "DUKE" TRADEMARK
APPLICATION

It is very important to file a rendition of your mark specific enough to steer clear of any other marks that are close. Perhaps JWE would have been better served by filing on a logo mark (i.e., the mark including a graphic and/or a special font) instead of the plain typed version of the mark to help avoid the oppositions filed by Duke University.

The downside of filing only on a logo is that the scope of protection is narrower and if the business owner changes the logo, the trademark application or registration on the old logo is probably no longer valid. To further JWE's case, JWE's trademark attorney tried to distinguish his client's trademark application from Duke University's marks by mentioning the connection of DUKE to John Wayne in the description of the goods. Specifically, the trademark attorney stated that the goods were used "in connection with indicia denoting the late internationally-known movie star John Wayne, who is also known as Duke."

This "in connection with" limitation of the goods is often overlooked, but can work wonders. In the case of JWE's trademark application on DUKE, the Examining Attorney at the Trademark Office accepted the application with the context of the goods being marketed in connection with John Wayne, who is known as "Duke." Therefore, even when a trademark application appears doomed, a clever trademark attorney may find a way to salvage it.

Since the oppositions against JWE's trademark applications were dismissed, DUKE Bourbon is still being offered for sale and Duke University does not appear to have sued for infringement. It may very well be that going forward the University will tolerate JWE's use of DUKE in the marketplace for certain goods as long as it is very clear that it is in connection with John Wayne.

Lesson Learned: A trademark application can be okay with the Trademark Office, but that doesn't ensure safe use of the mark. Conversely, a trademark application can be disallowed by the Trademark Office or due to an opposition proceeding, but you still may be able to safely use the mark. Most importantly, sometimes the actual (real world) context in which the trademark will be used can and should be part of your trademark application to successfully register the mark.

When a dispute arises, the faster the parties understand the differences in how they market, usually the faster the dispute can be resolved.

In this battle of "Dukes," in my view, the likelihood of confusion of DUKE for Duke University and its apparel and other goods and services, and DUKE when in association with John Wayne is very small. In particular, it helps to have the imagery of John Wayne used on the bottle. In any event, JWE may be wishing that Duke University was still named Trinity College or Brown's Schoolhouse.

CHAPTER 3

HOORAY FOR THE RED, WHITE & BLUE: THE IMPORTANCE OF FIRST TO USE

In trademark law, the first user of a trademark is called the "senior user." The senior user has priority over any later user, known as the "junior user." This rule means that even if you are the first to file a trademark application, but you file after the senior user started its use of the mark, the senior user is the one entitled to the mark.[4] The case of *Tassel Ridge Winery, LLC v. WoodMill Winery, Inc.*, Case No. 5:11-CV-00066-RLV, 2013 WL 5567505 (W.D.N.C. Oct. 9, 2013) illustrates this rule.

Tassel Ridge Winery of Iowa was formed in 2004. The winery is in the tiny town of Leighton, which as of 2013 had a population of about 160. Iowa is not known for vineyards or wineries, especially due to its long, cold winters. However, Concord grapes will grow there and have been grown there, on and off, since the mid-nineteenth century.

In 2006, Tassel Ridge named its Concord blend RED, WHITE & BLUE. This name was part of a series of patriotic names for Tassel Ridge wines including STAR SPANGLED WHITE, AMERICAN MERLOT, AMERICAN CHARDONNAY and ROCKETS GLARE ROSÉ. Tassel Ridge applied for a COLA[5],

4 An exception to the "first to use" rule occurs if you file an intent to use (ITU) trademark application before a competitor starts using the same or substantially similar mark, even if that competitor used the mark before you used the mark. The ITU application will give you priority as long as you eventually use the mark and obtain the registration.

5 "COLA" stands for Certificate of Label Approval, issued by the Alcohol and Tobacco Tax and Trade Bureau (TTB), which is part of the U.S. Treasury Department. The issuance of a COLA means that the TTB has authorized the bottling or packaging of wine with the submitted label. No wine may be bottled, sold, or shipped in the United States without first obtaining a COLA. The TTB was previously known as the Bureau of Alcohol, Tobacco and Firearms (BATF or ATF).

which was granted on July 5, 2006. Shortly thereafter Tassel Ridge started selling its RED, WHITE & BLUE wine. On October 17, 2007, Tassel Ridge filed a federal trademark application on RED, WHITE & BLUE for use on wine, and registration was granted.

WoodMill Winery of North Carolina opened in about July 2005. WoodMill Winery is located in Vale, about one hour northwest of Charlotte. Apparently unknown to Tassel Ridge, WoodMill had the idea to sell a wine that is a blend of red and white grapes as well as blueberries. WoodMill also called its wine RED, WHITE & BLUE.

According to WoodMill's website, the founder's father, who was suffering from a heart condition, was inspired by an article he read about "the French paradox." This article stated that drinking a reasonable amount of red wine daily for a long time could reduce the likelihood of heart disease by up to 40 percent. This belief is somewhat supported by the Mayo Clinic which has found in its research that drinking red wine in moderation does appear to improve good cholesterol and reduce bad cholesterol. However, the Mayo Clinic also points out that most research into this subject has been done on animals, not people.[6] Additionally, blueberries are high in antioxidants, which are believed to help reduce bad cholesterol.[7]

WoodMill, it appears, incorporated blueberries as an ingredient into its wine to help fight heart disease. Because this wine was nonstandard, WoodMill had to obtain government approval of the formulation and process for production. It submitted an application to the Alcohol and Tobacco Tax and Trade Bureau (TTB) for the wine formulation on April 7, 2006,

---

6 www.mayoclinic.org/diseases-conditions/in-depth/red-wine/art-20048281
7 http://www.webmd.com/heart-disease/features/five-superfoods-for-heart#1

and obtained approval ten days later. Unfortunately, WoodMill did not submit its COLA application for the label approval until August 28, 2006. A timeline of key events is shown below.

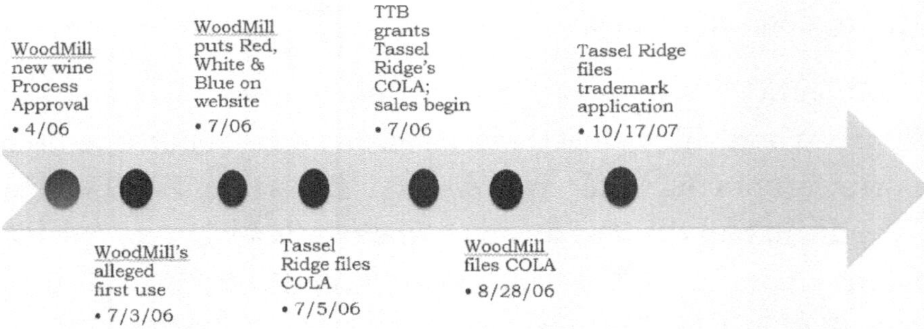

For about five years, Tassel Ridge and WoodMill were selling wine using the same name. Then, in 2011, Tassel Ridge became aware of WoodMill's wine, sending them a cease and desist letter. When WoodMill did not comply, Tassel Ridge filed suit against WoodMill for trademark infringement.

After a couple of years of litigation, Tassel Ridge asked the Court to grant summary judgment[8] against WoodMill. The basis was that both companies' marks (RED, WHITE & BLUE) and goods (wine) were the same, and that Tassel Ridge used the mark first.

In response to Tassel Ridge's motion for summary judgment, WoodMill claimed it had first sold its wine on July 3, 2006, before Tassel Ridge's first sale later that same month. The Court found that even if WoodMill had sales of its wine before Tassel Ridge had any sales, WoodMill's early sales were before WoodMill had approval of its COLA application.

8 "Summary judgment" refers to when a court decides a lawsuit without having a trial. A litigant can request (make a motion for) summary judgment when it thinks there are only legal issues, and no dispute about any important facts. If the court agrees, it will grant the motion for summary judgment and thus decide the case.

The Court stated the rule that the first user has priority, but that use must be lawful. WoodMill's sales of wine prior to receipt of the COLA were not considered lawful and thus, they didn't count.

WoodMill also claimed it was first to use the mark because it filed its April 2006 application for approval of its wine-making process, and because it used the name RED, WHITE & BLUE on its website before Tassel Ridge used the mark. However, "use" in a trademark sense comes from actual sales of wine. Merely advertising or submitting an application for approval of a wine-making process is not the same as sales of wine with the trademark on the label. Accordingly, these claimed uses didn't count either.

The Court found that Tassel Ridge was the senior user. Nevertheless, summary judgment was denied because a trial was needed to determine if there was infringement. WoodMill claimed its use of the mark RED, WHITE & BLUE was descriptive of its ingredients, and as such, it did not use the words as a trademark. This issue never got resolved because the parties settled shortly thereafter.

Lesson Learned: File a trademark application early. WoodMill may very well have been the first to conceive of the mark RED, WHITE & BLUE. It may even have been the first to put the mark on its website. However, WoodMill's mistake was making the mark public long before WoodMill lawfully sold wine with the RED, WHITE & BLUE label, and failing to file an ITU trademark application.

To protect its trademark rights, WoodMill should have filed an ITU trademark application before posting its mark on its website. Had WoodMill done so in April of 2006, before Tassel Ridge started selling its wine, WoodMill would have preserved its rights. However, once Tassel Ridge started selling wine with the mark on it, any trademark application by WoodMill would have been too late. In this situation, early filing of a trademark application probably would have avoided large expenses in trademark litigation.

CHAPTER 4

INFRINGEMENT ISN'T SEXY: IS YOUR WINE'S LABEL PROPERLY CLEARED?

Trademarks cover a word, slogan, phrase, logo, image, smell or sound when used in connection with a good or service, as we've seen in the cases of wine, spirits and clothing.

In contrast, copyrights cover a work, such as a picture, painting, literary work or a video from being copied. Although trademark and copyright can appear to overlap, they are separate and distinct types of protection. Ownership of a copyright on an image does not mean you own that image as a trademark, and ownership of a trademark that uses an image does not mean you own a copyright on the image.

In *Nova Wines, Inc. v. Adler Fels Winery, LLC*, 467 F. Supp. 2d 965 (N.D. Ca 2007), the Court faced this clash of copyright and trademark law as the parties argued about who could use nude photos of Marilyn Monroe on a wine label.

Even decades after Ms. Monroe's passing, Marilyn Monroe is still a household name. Born in 1926 in Los Angeles, Ms. Monroe was brought up by a single mother who struggled to care for her. Due to issues beyond her control, the young Norma Jean was raised in several foster homes and even spent time in an orphanage. Her childhood dream was to become an actress.

Norma Jean started out as a model as well as an actress appearing in small movie roles. In 1949, just before she hit it big, she did her first nude photo shoot. The next year she was cast as the lead in *All About Eve*, and signed a multiyear contract with 20th Century-Fox. When it was discovered that Ms. Monroe had posed nude, her popularity increased. Later in her career, she became the centerfold in Playboy magazine's first issue.

Perhaps Marilyn's best-known photo is the one where her dress is billowing up while she's standing over a subway grate in New York City. This photo was done as part of a publicity shot for *The Seven Year Itch*, in which she starred. Ms. Monroe also starred in *Some Like It Hot*, for which she earned a Golden Globe for Best Actress.

In 1962, while Ms. Monroe was filming a skinny-dipping scene for *Something's Got to Give*, the press were allowed to take photos and Life Magazine eventually published some. Later that year, she died of an apparent drug overdose at the age of 36.

With multiple sources having obtained nude photos of the late star, a clash of rights was bound to happen. The *Nova Wines, Inc. v. Adler Fels Winery, LLC* case illustrates how Ms. Monroe's likeness was used in a situation where trademark rights turned out to be superior to copyright.

In 1989, Nova Wines, a St. Helena, California, winery, obtained a license from the estate of Marilyn Monroe to use her name and likeness on their wine. After receiving it, they continued using her likeness for the next 20 years.

Eventually, Tom Kelly Studios ("TKS"), which held copyright to the 1949 nude photos, approached Nova Wines to see if they wanted to use them on their wine labels and logo. Nova Wines, believing that the TTB was not likely to approve a wine label with nudity on it, went ahead with the photos but with a "modesty overlay" to cover Ms. Monroe's breasts and buttocks. After the TTB approved the label with the overlay, Nova Wines licensed the photos from TKS in 2004.

However, the use of the overlay did not sit well with TKS's artistic integrity, so TKS terminated its license with Nova Wines. Fortunately for Nova Wines, Ms. Monroe had multiple nude photo shoots. Nova Wines then went to Playboy and licensed their photos. The Playboy photos (with an overlay) were then used on the wine label and wine sales continued.

Meanwhile, TKS tried to license its nude photos to another winery. However, Nova Wine's counsel stepped in to prevent this, stating that it would be a trademark infringement. Undaunted, TKS found Adler Fels Winery, located in Santa Rosa, California, which took a license for use of the nude photos on their wine labels. Shortly after Adler Fels started using TKS's photos, Nova Wines sued for trademark infringement.

Adler Fels argued that because it was using TKS's nude photos, and because TKS had a signed release from Ms. Monroe (obtained decades earlier) allowing use of the photos and her name, Adler Fels could put these photos on their wine labels.

In contrast, Nova Wines argued that for years, it was the only seller of wines with photos of Marilyn Monroe on the label. As such, it owned trademark and trade dress rights in her name and likeness on wine regardless of who owned copyright.

The Court agreed with Nova Wines and granted a preliminary injunction ordering Adler Fels to refrain from using the pictures of Ms. Monroe on the label. The reason was that Nova Wines had superior trademark rights in use of images of Ms. Monroe on wine making TKS's copyright ownership of the nude photos irrelevant.

Remember, trademark rights are defined not only by the word(s) and/or image(s) that form the mark, but also by the goods and/or services with which they are used. Generally, the first user of a mark on the goods has superior rights. Nova Wines was the first user of images of Ms. Monroe on wine.

This was an expensive lesson for Adler Fels, which estimated that revenue from the initial year's release of 15,000 cases would be $4,000,000. The actual out-of-pocket expense was about $140,000 on product development and bottling of the first 2,000 preordered bottles, plus a lot of attorney's fees.

Lesson Learned: Adler Fels could have avoided these problems by initiating a good trademark or trade dress clearance search and opinion. All wine has to have a label and a name. The name and label art should be cleared with trademark counsel before finalizing the label, and certainly before marketing. The same is true for any new product, service or business name. It should be cleared by counsel.

CHAPTER 5

DUCK, DUCK, GOOSE: IF YOU GET INTO A SQUABBLE, SETTLE IT CAREFULLY

In 2001, Duckhorn Wine Company of St. Helena, California and Duck Walk Vineyards of Water Mill, New York accused one another of trademark infringement. First, Duck Walk filed suit against Duckhorn in New York in the case of *Duck Walk Vineyards, Inc. v. St. Helena Wine Co., d/b/a Duckhorn Vineyards*, Case No. 01-cv-4896 (E.D.N.Y. 2001). Duck Walk, in essence, said: "Duckhorn is too close to Duck Walk. Tell Duckhorn to change its name."

Then, Duckhorn countersued for trademark infringement. After about two years of legal wrangling and discovery, the parties finally settled in 2003. The terms of that settlement would later become very important, as it impacted a later case between the two wineries: *Duckhorn Wine Company v. Duck Walk Vineyards Inc.*, Case No. 2:13-cv-01642 (E.D.N.Y. 2015).

Duckhorn Wine Company was formed in 1976 in the Napa Valley wine region of California and released its first wine under the DUCKHORN label in 1980. Since then, Duckhorn has released a variety of wines under the DUCKHORN label using duck-themed names and duck images. Along the way, Duckhorn obtained a federal registration on DUCKHORN VINEYARDS for wines. In 2000, Duckhorn also filed on just the name DUCKHORN for wines. This was a smart move to broaden its rights.

Nearly 20 years later, Duck Walk Vineyards was founded in 1994 in the famed Hamptons on Long Island. Given that there are a lot of ducks in this region, it is easy to see why Duck Walk picked its name, but Duck Walk never applied for or registered its name with the U.S. Trademark Office.

A search of the Trademark Office registry showed that there are other registrations using the word DUCK, where the mark is two words and the goods are wine:

DUCK POND	registered in 1994;
DUCK SHACK	registered in 2008;
DUCK TAPE	registered in 2010; and
DUCK DOWN	registered in 2014.

Possibly, if push came to shove, Duck Walk could have continued to use the "Duck Walk" name, and of course possibly it would have lost the 2001 lawsuit. We don't know since the parties settled the matter, and there is always uncertainty in any lawsuit. Continuing to fight would have cost significant additional money and been a huge risk as there are no guarantees in litigation. So Duck Walk signed the 2003 settlement in which it agreed to limit distribution under the DUCK WALK label and duck images to no more than 84,000 gallons per year, with no more than half the production being sold outside its tristate area (New York, New Jersey and Connecticut). Moreover, Duck Walk had to put its appellation[9] "on the front label."

The 2003 settlement required Duck Walk to put the agreed-upon appellations "The Hamptons," "South Hamptons," "South Fork" or "Long Island" *on the front label.* These appellations do not have the panache of "Napa" or "California," or various other popular viticultural[10] regions, so any winery owner would probably want to put them on the back label where they would

9 An "appellation" is the name of the geographic area or viticultural region where the grapes were grown.

10 A "*viticultural* region" or area is specifically a government defined wine grape–growing area.

be less noticeable. However, the 2003 settlement was fairly reasonable for both parties *at the time.*

However, as the winery started to expand, Duck Walk's perspective may have changed (perhaps because it found the settlement too restrictive). In 2007, it opened another location on Long Island. Additionally, possibly after taking a closer look at the term "front label" in the agreement, Duck Walk came up with a plan: Submit a COLA to the Bureau of Alcohol, Tobacco and Firearms (BATF) and switch what would normally be the "front label" (the one with the wine name and pretty picture) with the "back label" (the one with the Surgeon General's warning). Then the new "front label," as approved by the BATF, would have the appellation and satisfy the agreement.

Duckhorn took exception to these changes and, in 2013, filed another law suit against Duck Walk, this time for breach of the 2003 settlement agreement.

In the 2013 lawsuit, the parties argued over what constitutes the "front label" and the "back label." Duck Walk asserted that the front label, under the 2003 settlement, is whatever is termed "front label" in the COLA application, while Duckhorn asserted that the "front label" is what the industry understands to be the front label (the bigger label with the pretty picture).

From a review of the key language in the 2003 settlement agreement, most likely the term "front label" means the industry standard front label. The language of the agreement refers to the BATF only with respect to the geographic designation:

> The words “The Hamptons”, “South Hamptons”, “South Fork” and/or “Long Island” or other geographic designation of like import as may be approved by BATF (the prefatory language) shall be added on the front label of all of the Gross Production.

Presumably, to bolster its argument that the front label is whatever label Duck Walk designates to be the front label in its COLA application, Duck Walk’s website showed the label with the Surgeon General’s warning and appellation facing the viewer. The pretty picture that is usually on the front label faces away as shown below on its Duck Walk wines.

2013 Cabernet

2013 Merlot

After another two years of legal wrangling, the parties settled again. This time they clarified the 2003 settlement. Their new agreement stated that what the BATF defined as the “brand label” is deemed the “front label.” According to BATF, the brand label is “the principal display panel that is most likely to be displayed…under normal and customary conditions of display for retail sale.”

Lesson Learned: When you select a mark, not only should you do a trademark search, but you need to also carefully consider the search results and whether or not you are too far into the "gray zone." The gray zone is where it is possible for you to think your mark is fine, but also possible for an earlier trademark user (here Duckhorn) to think your mark infringes. While you may be able to settle a trademark dispute if it arises, what you have to give up in order to settle may be more than you can live with, over time.

CHAPTER 6

HALLOWEEN SURPRISE: WATCH OUT FOR FAMOUS TRADEMARKS

Assuming you have done a clearance search at the U.S. Trademark Office website and found that there are no registered trademarks that appear close to your proposed wine name, are you now safe to use it?

Not always. In the case of *C&N Corporation dba Door Peninsula Winery v. Gregory Kane and Illinois River Winery, Inc.*, Case No. 12-C-0257 (E.D.Wis., 2013), both parties had competing trademark applications on HALLOWINE for wine. While Door Peninsula was the first to use the mark, Illinois River was the first to file a trademark application. Both applications failed, as explained below.

Door Peninsula, founded in 1974, is located in Door County, Wisconsin which is known for its cherries. Door County sits on a long peninsula extending generally northward into Lake Michigan, about an hour's drive from Green Bay. From its humble origins with its cherry and other fruit-flavored wines, Door Peninsula has grown significantly to include a vineyard, a restaurant and a distillery for making liquor.

Illinois River is located in North Utica, Illinois, roughly an hour and a half southwest of Chicago. Illinois River started as a vineyard; then in 1998, the winery was founded. Like Door Peninsula, Illinois River has several fruit wines and some creative wine names, like FUNNY BUNNY.

Door Peninsula's Hallowine Is First

According to Door Peninsula, in 1998, it started selling a spiced wine called HALLOWINE. The bottle used orange and black colors and prominently featured a jack-o'-lantern on the label. The intent was evidently to sell it during the fall and capitalize on Halloween.

Illinois River's Hallowine Is Second

According to Illinois River, in April 2005, it started selling a spiced wine called HALLOWINE. Its bottle also had a Halloween theme using orange and black colors and a scarecrow figure with a jack-o'-lantern head.

The two competing bottles are shown below.

Door Peninsula's HALLOWINE

Illinois River's HalloWine

Both companies filed trademark applications on HALLOWINE. Illinois River filed its application in March 2006, seven months before Door Peninsula. Since the first to use appeared to be Door Peninsula, by many years, it was likely that Door Peninsula would win the battle. But before the Trademark Office would allow Door Peninsula's mark to get registered, Door Peninsula would have to file an opposition and prove that it was the first to use the mark.

Door Peninsula's Opposition to Illinois River's "Hallowine" Trademark Application

Door Peninsula did just that. In 2008, the Trademark Trial and Appeals Board (TTAB) found that Door Peninsula was the first to use and sustained the opposition, preventing Illinois River from registering HALLOWINE. Illinois River's application then was abandoned.

However, just because an application is abandoned does not mean that the trademark owner has given up on its rights or has no rights. Undaunted, Illinois River continued to sell its HALLOWINE product.

After Illinois River's application was abandoned, the Trademark Office published Door Peninsula's application on HALLOWINE to see if anyone would oppose it. Publication in the Official Gazette (OG) is normal procedure when the Trademark Office approves of the application. Publication gives other companies an opportunity to oppose registration if they believe they will be harmed by it.

Large companies, and some smaller ones, review the published trademark applications in the OG as part of protecting their own marks. One of those large companies that undoubtedly watches the OG is E. & J. Gallo.

E. & J. Gallo's Opposition Against Door Peninsula's "Hallowine" Trademark Application

When Gallo saw HALLOWINE, it filed an opposition. This may have surprised Door Peninsula. How could HALLOWINE, sold with a Halloween-themed label and coming from a winery in Wisconsin, be confused with GALLO? But, when you are dealing with famous marks like GALLO, you must be wary.

The Trademark Office had allowed Door Peninsula's application to pass to publication without rejecting it. Presumably Gallo opposed because GALLO and "Hallo" rhyme and have the same letters except for the "G" and "H." Further, if one says, "Gallo wine," that rhymes with HALLOWINE. Gallo probably considered that as well.

The parties, Gallo and Door Peninsula, agreed to suspend the proceedings for a total of about 14 months for settlement negotiations. Probably due to settlement, Door Peninsula abandoned its federal application, but continued to sell HALLOWINE. In fact, in 2011, shortly after this TTAB proceeding ended, Door Peninsula filed an application on DOOR COUNTY HALLOWINE with "Hallowine" in a special font. The application passed to registration. It is unclear why Gallo allowed registration and use of this mark, but most likely it was a business decision Gallo made to resolve the opposition.

While Door Peninsula was capable of fighting (it did so against Illinois River), it wisely chose not to take on Gallo. Door Peninsula probably did not want to spend tens or hundreds of thousands of dollars in litigation.

It is important to understand that even though a trademark owner may abandon an application or never file for a trademark registration, the owner will still have "common law" trademark rights merely by using the trademark. These rights cover the geographic area in which the mark is used (as opposed to rights from a federal trademark registration, which extend throughout the U.S. even if use is only in a small area).

Door Peninsula Sues Illinois River for Trademark Infringement

Door Peninsula's successful opposition to Illinois River's trademark application was not the last of Illinois River's headaches. In 2012, Door Peninsula, as first user of the mark, sued Illinois River in federal court, alleging trademark infringement of its DOOR COUNTY HALLOWINE registration and its common law rights in HALLOWINE. Reading between the lines of the case, it appears that the defendant, Illinois River, believed that "Hallowine" was commonly used in the wine industry. An internet search on "Hallowine" revealed several late October wine events having essentially that name. Or, due to both parties failing to register "Hallowine," Illinois River believed Door Peninsula did not have a mark any more.

Surely one company cannot claim exclusive rights for an unregistered name that is commonly used in promoting wine-related events? Moreover, both companies had abandoned their federal applications on that name. Notwithstanding, the Trial Court decided in favor of Door Peninsula, and awarded over $500,000 in damages (representing Illinois River's profits on HALLOWINE).

Illinois River then appealed. As in the vast majority of appeals, the Appellate Court affirmed the Trial Court's decision. However, in spite of losing in the Trademark Office and in court, Illinois River still did not quit. After the Trial Judge entered a permanent injunction against Illinois River forbidding use of "Hallowine" or a colorable variation thereof, Illinois River tried to use similar names including "HalloW" and "Hallow Wine," as shown below.

HalloW

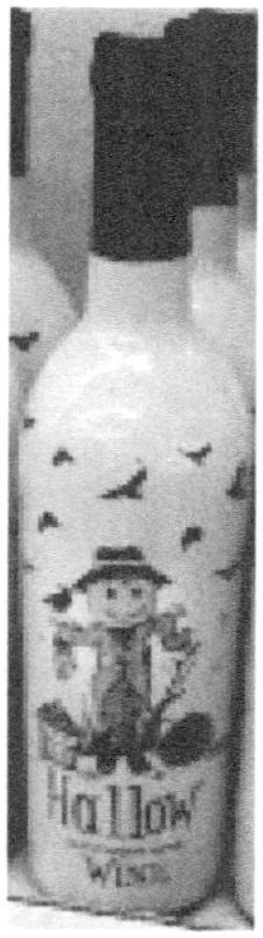

Hallow Wine

Door Peninsula did not take well to that effort to circumvent the Court's decision and brought a motion for contempt of the Court's injunction order. The Court sided with Door Peninsula and hit Illinois River with over $100,000 more in sanctions. Adding to the previous damages awarded, the total was now over $600,000.

All of these proceedings were expensive. Door Peninsula did not necessarily make much money back for fighting in the Trademark Office and in the courts, even assuming that it got paid all of the money it was awarded.

For Illinois River, this was a financial disaster. It filed Chapter 11 (reorganization proceedings) in bankruptcy court. The damages it owed Door Peninsula were a large portion of the debt and possibly the impetus for the bankruptcy filing. The bankruptcy proceeding itself was expensive. Door Peninsula (C&N Corporation) asked the Bankruptcy Court to convert Illinois River's Chapter 11 proceeding into a Chapter 7 proceeding where Illinois River would be completely liquidated, and the Court granted that motion. Illinois River, however, wanted to stay in business and so apparently worked out a deal with Door Peninsula to avoid liquidation.

Lesson Learned: There are a few lessons here: If you have a good mark that appears to have value in and of itself (due to cleverness or the like), you should be prepared to fight for it. In addition, when you select a trademark, watch out for famous marks. They can come from out of left field to bite you. Sometimes registration, although very often desirable, is not the best path. If you are second to use a mark, then you may be best off letting it go. Evaluating trademark rights can be complex with a lot of factors to consider. The best advice is to not let ego, emotions or visions of profits blind you from exercising good business judgment.

CHAPTER 7

IS IT ALL ABOUT LOCATION? GEOGRAPHICAL NAMES CAN BE HARD TO PROTECT

Many wineries and vineyards use geographic or viticultural names in their marks. This often sounds like a good idea. A search of the federal trademark registry on "Sonoma" included at least 184 applications and registrations using "Sonoma"[11] as part of a trademark for "wine" or wine-related goods or services. The first winery that registered a mark using "Sonoma" was L. Foppiano Wine Co. in 1948 for the mark SONOMA GOLD wines with first use in 1935. The mark was registered in what we call "stylized form," meaning the type font or style is special:

SONOMA
GOLD

The problem with using a geographic name is that it can be hard to enforce, i.e., to stop later users of the same geographic name. For example, SONOMA CREEK, SONOMA VINEYARDS, SONOMA-LOEB, GALLO SONOMA, SONOMA CUVEE, and SONOMA RIDGE are all examples of federal registrations using "Sonoma" for wine. With so many users of similar names, how does one distinguish its winery or vineyard in the mind of a consumer?

11 The search was conducted in March 2016 for any federal trademark application or registration (live or dead) having the word "Sonoma" in the mark, and goods or services having the word "wine." There actually may be a much higher number of applications and registrations using "Sonoma" for wine-related goods or services. This is because the description of goods or services for some wine-related products or services need not include the word "wine," such as a corkscrew.

Building a strong and enforceable mark is much easier if the name is not geographic. A good example of the problems that can result in enforcing geographic marks is the case of *Leelanau Wine Cellars, Ltd. v. Black & Red, Inc.*, 502 F.3d 504 (6th Cir. 2007).

After decades of use, the Michigan winery Leelanau Wine Cellars (LWC) thought it had a strong mark. Leelanau is a viticultural region and county on the Upper Peninsula (U.P.) of Michigan.

LWC is in the town of Omena, located on the coast of the Grand Traverse Bay of Lake Michigan. The winery has a waterfront tasting room for the more than 30 varietals of grapes it grows in this cold, snowy wine region, which gets an average annual snowfall of 17 feet.

Michigan's Leelanau Peninsula, showing Omena and Suttons Bay on shores of Grand Traverse Bay

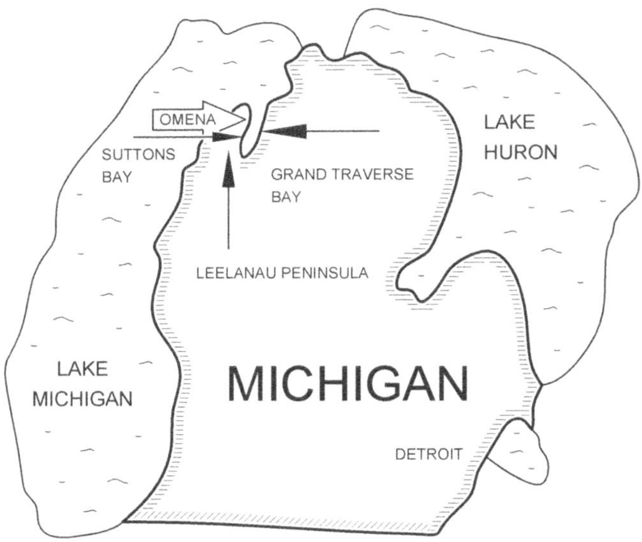

Leelanau Wine Cellars Is First

LWC first sold wine under the name "Leelanau Wine Cellars" in 1977. About 20 years later, LWC filed for federal registration on "Leelanau Cellars" and the trademark office granted the registration.

Chateau de Leelanau Is Second

In 1990, Black & Red (B&R) started growing fruit, including grapes, and, in 1999, making wine in the Leelanau viticultural region. B&R is located in Suttons Bay, which is also on the Grand Traverse Bay, south of Omena. In 2000, B&R changed its name to "Chateau de Leelanau Vineyard and Winery" and started selling its wine.

Leelanau Cellars

Chateau De Leelanau

In October 2000, LWC sent B&R a cease and desist letter accusing them of infringement. Specifically, LWC asserted that B&R's use of the word "Leelanau" in its mark infringed LWC's trademark rights. In May 2001, LWC sued B&R for trademark infringement.

Notwithstanding the lawsuit and LWC's registration on LEELANAU CELLARS, B&R applied for and obtained a registration on CHATEAU DE LEELANAU VINEYARD

AND WINERY. In 2002, the Judge found that it was likely B&R infringed. Then, to LWC's horror, the Judge changed his mind.

Why the change? In order for a company to have a trademark, the mark must identify a single source of goods or services in the buyers' minds. If the primary meaning to the public is a place (rather than a company), then the mark is geographically descriptive. Back in 1977, when LWC first opened, buyers would have been more likely to believe that the "Leelanau Cellars" mark indicated that the wine cellar was located in Leelanau rather than indicating a specific company.

A geographically descriptive mark is not an enforceable trademark, unless and until the trademark owner establishes "secondary meaning." This means that consumers now identify the geographic name with the source of the goods or services rather than simply the location where the goods or services originate.

Secondary meaning is established by showing that one has used the mark for a long time and/or has a lot of sales and advertising. It can also be established by a survey of potential customers, showing they consider the name to identify a particular company rather than a geographic location of the company.

When the Judge compared the two marks: LEELANAU CELLARS and CHATEAU DE LELANAU VINEYARD AND WINERY, the only thing in common was the word "Leelanau." That word is geographic. Even though LWC had been using its mark for over 20 years and had a federal trademark registration, and even had established secondary meaning in the mark, the Judge found that the term "Leelanau," alone, was not protectable by LWC.

The secondary meaning was established by the whole mark (LEELANAU CELLARS), not the single word "Leelanau." Because the only word in common in the two marks had geographic significance and no trademark significance, the Judge found no likelihood of infringement.

So LWC appealed and the Court of Appeals affirmed the Judge, albeit for a different reason. The Appellate Court said that the LWC mark was not strong and that the marks were not that similar. It also noted that B&R sold its wine mostly on its premises through its tasting room, so consumers were not likely to be confused about whether they were buying from LWC or B&R.

Lesson Learned: Descriptiveness and secondary meaning can be complicated concepts. The simple point is that if you adopt a geographic business or product name, you are hamstringing enforcement of your mark. Therefore, when adopting a mark, it is better to avoid geographic names.

CHAPTER 8

MEANING WITH A TWIST: WHEN TRADEMARKS ARE MISDESCRIPTIVE

Vintners, viticulturists and oenologists[12] (oh my!) would all agree that appellation is critical in the wine industry. The appellation gives rise to an expectation of quality and taste. In the same way, a trademark gives rise to an expectation of quality and taste. Whether you like Heineken®, Coors®, Michelob®, Miller® or Budweiser® makes a difference to many.

Sometimes trademarks and appellations conflict. Does a wine product with "Chablis" in its name have to have the legal minimum amount of grapes grown in the Chablis region of France? Not always, according to the case of *The Institut National Des Appellations D'Origine v. Vintners International Company, Inc.*, 958 F.2d 1574 (Fed. Cir. 1992).

In 1988, Vintners International Company ("Vintners") applied for a registration in the U.S. Trademark Office on "Chablis with a Twist." The wine product sold using this mark did not contain any grapes from the Chablis region of France. Nevertheless, the Trademark Office allowed the application.

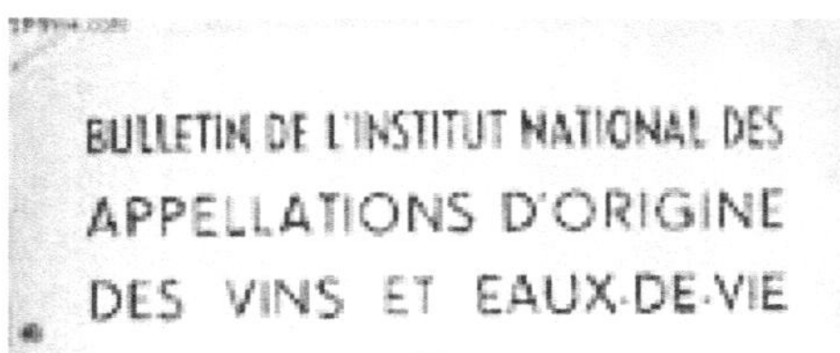
BULLETIN DE L'INSTITUT NATIONAL DES
APPELLATIONS D'ORIGINE
DES VINS ET EAUX-DE-VIE

The Institut National Des Appellations D'Origine ("The Institut") is an organization that enforces France's appellations.

12 A "vintner" is a wine-seller or a winemaker. A "viticulturist" is a person who grows grapes, especially for winemaking. An "oenologist" or "enologist" is one who studies the science of wine and winemaking.

The Institut opposed Vintners' trademark application, mainly on the grounds that the mark was geographically misdescriptive since the label said "Chablis" but there were no Chablis grapes in the wine.

The BATF (which is now the TTB) regulations classified "Chablis" as a type or class of wine that has geographic significance. Labeling a white wine as "Chablis," if produced anywhere other than the Chablis region of France, is prohibited unless the place of origin is shown "in direct conjunction therewith."

The BATF approved "Chablis with a Twist" because the place of origin, California, was in the tagline–"California White Wine with Natural Citrus"–and was "as conspicuous as the word Chablis" in the BATF's opinion.

Trademarks, like appellations, are not allowed to be geographically misdescriptive. Generally, a business cannot call its sunglasses PARIS SUNGLASSES if the goods are not from Paris. The name would be understood by a consumer to mean the place Paris, France. In this situation, the use of "Paris" would mislead a significant portion of consumers into thinking the sunglasses were from Paris.

The Trademark Office has different standards than the BATF. While Vintners had the word "California" on the label, it sought to register CHABLIS WITH A TWIST as the trademark. As is obvious, the word "California" is not in this phrase. Nevertheless, both the TTAB and the Examining Attorney found this trademark to be fine and not misdescriptive.

However, the Institut did not give up. It appealed to the United States Court of Appeals for the Federal Circuit. The

Appellate Court determined that in the U.S., in addition to being an appellation, "Chablis" was considered to mean a type of white wine. Because "Chablis" had this significant additional meaning, the mark was not considered geographically misdescriptive. Moreover, use of the phrase "with a Twist" indicated to consumers that there was something different about this "Chablis." Therefore, Vintners' was allowed to keep its trademark registration.

Lesson Learned: The meaning(s) of a word or phrase can have a critical influence affecting how a trademark is viewed by consumers. This case could very well have ended differently had the trademark application sought registration of a mark such as PURE WHITE CHABLIS, or had been in a French court. In any event, this case points out that in trademarks, one must consider how consumers who are located in the U.S. will interpret the trademark.

CHAPTER 9

THE WRATHFUL GRAPES OF NAPA: A COLA DOESN'T ENSURE SAFE TRADEMARK USE

Providers of goods and services often use descriptive terms, including geographic terms or place names, to inform consumers about the origin, nature or quality of their goods and services. Napa Valley is, without a doubt, one of the most recognized and highly regarded viticultural regions in the U.S. Therefore, it is no surprise that a winery would go to great lengths to be associated with the Napa Valley, even if its grapes do not come from there.

The Trademark Office will not register marks that they consider misleading. In addition, the TTB sets standards for use of geographic terms or viticultural regions for wine. Unfortunately for the Bronco Wine Company, their efforts to use the term "Napa" in their trademarks NAPA RIDGE and NAPA CREEK WINERY were found to mislead consumers. The case of *Bronco Wine Co. v. Jolly*, 29 Cal.Rptr.3d 462 (2005) explains why.

Bronco Wine Company was founded in 1973 in Ceres, California, which is just south of Modesto. It is the largest vineyard owner and the fifth largest winery in the U.S.

Wanting to keep its costs down, Bronco decided to use non-Napa grapes while, at the same time, putting the name "Napa" on its wine label. The problem Bronco faced was that California law, since 1986, prohibited use of the word "Napa" (or the name of any federally recognized viticultural area within Napa County) in a brand name unless the wine is made with a specified percentage of grapes grown in Napa.[13]

To that end, Bronco spent quite a bit of money to acquire brand names that had "Napa" in them prior to the 1986 law (Section 25241) expecting the use of "Napa" to be grandfathered in and thus be legally okay. These pre-1986 marks included NAPA RIDGE and NAPA CREEK WINERY, whose previous owners had obtained COLAs from the BATF[14] for their wine bottle labels. However, what was not grandfathered in under California law was Bronco's use of these marks.

The NAPA RIDGE mark, owned by Beringer Vineyards, was purchased by Bronco along with its federal registration (for use on wines) for $42 million.[15] Bronco also purchased the mark NAPA CREEK WINERY and its federal trademark registration from another winery that had used the mark since before the 1986 law. Bronco then used its plant on the outskirts of Napa to bottle and label its wines with the NAPA RIDGE and NAPA CREEK marks.

While Bronco had stopped using grapes from Napa in its NAPA RIDGE and NAPA CREEK WINERY wines, this did not stop the BATF from issuing COLAs to Bronco's

13 California Business and Professions Code ("Cal. B&P") Section 25241.
14 The BATF or ATF became the TTB in 2003.
15 Paul Franson, "Napa Ridge Winery Gains a Home to Match Its Presence," *Wine Business Monthly*, August 2002.

wines, as the true appellation of origin of the grapes appeared somewhere on the label.

As is obvious, the very purpose of the 1986 California law was to stop wine companies who did not use a significant amount of Napa grapes from using "Napa" in their trademarks or their appellation. When the California Department of Alcoholic Beverage Control threatened Bronco for the "Napa" labeling, Bronco challenged the law in court.

To best understand this case, it's important to know some additional trademark principles. Trademark law will protect a word or phrase depending on where it falls on the following spectrum: generic, descriptive, suggestive, or arbitrary/fanciful.

Generic terms (e.g., "wine" for wine) can never be a trademark.

Descriptive terms (e.g., "tasty" for a red wine) describe a quality or characteristic of the goods. Descriptive terms initially are not protectable as trademarks. After sufficient time of advertising and/or sales, the trademark owner may be able to establish "secondary meaning" and if so, the mark is protectable.

"Secondary meaning" refers to consumers seeing the term as a trademark (an indication of source) and not as a description of a quality of the goods.

Geographic terms such as "Napa Valley" are treated as a form of descriptive mark. Therefore, protection of a geographic mark requires the user to establish "secondary meaning." Marks using just a surname are also treated as descriptive marks.

Suggestive marks have some remote connection to the goods, but still do not give away what the goods are and do not give away any quality of the goods. For example, the word "ocean," when used for a pool company name, has some relation to pools in that both (oceans and pools) contain water, but "ocean" does not describe a characteristic or quality of pools.

Arbitrary marks are existing words or phrases that have nothing to do with the goods, e.g., APPLE for a computer. Fanciful marks are made-up terms, e.g., XEROX (made up from the word "xerographic").

Suggestive or arbitrary/fanciful marks are considered inherently distinctive trademarks that are immediately protectable.

With these definitions in mind, Bronco's mark NAPA CREEK WINERY is a geographically descriptive mark. However, Bronco sold and advertised sufficient wine using this mark to establish secondary meaning. Therefore, it was considered protectable as a trademark. And while NAPA RIDGE sounds like a geographic place (in fact, it was made-up), it was arguably a fanciful mark.[16] But the story doesn't end here.

Although the Trademark Office may be fine with a mark, the trademark user also has to consider state and federal statutes concerning geographic names. This is true even if the user has been granted a COLA from the TTB approving such use.

16 Bear in mind that NAPA RIDGE may sound geographic to consumers, and so arguably is geographically descriptive. But, there is no place called "Napa Ridge," and so it is not descriptive. Moreover, Bronco undoubtedly had sufficient time of use, sales and advertising to establish secondary meaning.

Since the sale of wines containing a mark with the word "Napa" required Napa grapes be used under California's Section 25241, Bronco had to challenge this law to continue to sell under its "Napa" trademarks.

Bronco challenged the law on several grounds, arguing that the state law improperly limited its First Amendment right to free speech. But the Court rejected Bronco's free speech argument because use of a mark on goods (wine) is commercial speech, and commercial speech may be legislated much more significantly than noncommercial speech. Further, the Court concluded that use of the word "Napa" rendered Bronco's speech inherently misleading, since its grapes did not come from Napa.

Bronco then argued that Section 25241 wrongly impinged on the federal government's authority to regulate interstate commerce, so it was unconstitutional. This argument was unsuccessful too. The Court said that California's legitimate interest in protecting the value of the Napa appellation, as well as protecting its consumers from misleading product labels, outweighed any incidental encroachment upon federal law. Further, trademark law and appellation regulations are two different sets of rules.

Ultimately, Bronco lost its challenge and was required to comply with California law (in addition to federal law). However, the Court's ruling did not prohibit Bronco from using the NAPA RIDGE and NAPA CREEK WINERY names altogether. The Court simply said that if you're going to use these names, you had better be telling the truth! In other words, you had better be using Napa grapes.

For these reasons, Bronco ultimately started using Napa-grown grapes and revised its trademark registrations to change the goods from "wines" to "wine derived 75% or more from grapes grown in Napa County, California."

Lesson Learned: The lessons gained from this unsuccessful challenge include the following points:

- Geographically descriptive marks and other descriptive marks, which may seem appealing from a marketing standpoint, can be difficult to protect.
- Protection for descriptive and geographically descriptive marks is especially difficult early on (as in the first five years) in the use of the mark. They can also remain difficult after this time, even if secondary meaning is established.
- If using a geographically descriptive mark, make sure it is accurate.
- It is important to comply with all applicable state and federal laws.
- Obtaining a COLA (or other government regulatory approval) does not ensure that you have a valid trademark.

CHAPTER 10

DON'T JUST WINE ABOUT IT: WINE VERSUS BEER AND LIQUOR NAMES

Naming a new wine or any product or service is tricky. Not only should one avoid names already taken by another company, but one should also consider watching out for names that may be similar to other related products and services.

For example, the name of a beer or hard alcohol can stand in the way of use and registration of a mark for wine. In fact, the name of many other products or services can present an issue depending upon several factors, which are fact-specific, as demonstrated in the following two contrasting results at Trademark Trials and Appeals Board (TTAB) proceedings: Bell's Brewery's opposition to Bell Hill's trademark application, and Franciscan Vineyards, Inc.'s opposition to BeauxKat Enterprises LLC trademark application.

Bell's Brewery vs. Bell Hill Vineyards

Around 2006, a start-up California winery named itself Bell Hill Vineyards. At that time, Ms. Julia Martelli, owner and manager of Bell Hill, filed a federal intent-to-use trademark application on BELL HILL for "packaged wine." Whether or not she had done a trademark search, we do not know.

Ms. Martelli did a good job on the application itself. The Examining Attorney at the U.S. Trademark Office found the application to be in order. There were no marks on the federal registry that presented any issues as far as the Examining Attorney was concerned. Therefore, as is standard Trademark Office procedure, the application was published for opposition by third parties.

Bell's Brewery grew out of a homebrew beer shop formed by Larry Bell in Kalamazoo, Michigan. Bell's Brewery had filed a trademark application in 1994 claiming first use of BELL'S in 1985 but that application later was abandoned. Subsequently, in 1998, Bell's Brewery filed again on BELL'S for beer. After a five-year ordeal, Bell's Brewery got a registration in 2003. Persistence can pay off.

Bell's Brewery saw the BELL HILL trademark application and opposed issuance of the registration. Bell's Brewery, the first to use, argued that consumers would be confused by the name BELL HILL on wine because BELL'S was already being used for beer. Also, Bell's logo was registered in 2003, which preceded Bell Hill's use. The two marks, BELL'S registered logo and BELL HILL (as used on its wine label) are as follows:

Bell's Brewery's logo

Bell Hill's logo

The standard for trademark infringement is whether it is likely that consumers, aware of the first (senior) trademark owner's brand, would be confused when they see the second (junior) user's brand with a similar name on their product or service. The issue comes down to whether or not consumers would believe the junior user's goods or services were produced or sponsored by the senior user.

As mentioned in the chapter on JWE versus Duke University, an opposition proceeding in the Trademark Office is like a lawsuit. One important difference, however, is that instead of a judge and jury, the TTAB decides the case. In the *Bell's Brewery v. Bell Hill* opposition, the TTAB looked mostly at four factors of an eight-factor test for determining whether there was a likelihood of confusion between the two marks:

First, how close are the two marks? The TTAB said that BELL'S for beer was one word with a picture of bells next to it. This picture reinforced the meaning of the word as relating to bells. While BELL HILL had the word "bell" in common, it had a different meaning: BELL HILL sounds like a place.

Second, how close are the goods? The TTAB said that beer and wine are related because both are alcoholic beverages and both are often sold in the same stores. Also, they are occasionally produced by the same company.

Third, how strong is the first trademark? The TTAB said that the BELL'S mark was not famous and was not a strong mark. Surnames are not strong marks, unless there has been a lot of sales and advertising using the name, e.g., as in the case of McDONALD'S.

Fourth, are consumers sophisticated and/or is this type of good an "impulse" buy, or is it purchased after a lot of thought? The TTAB concluded that wine was generally not an impulse buy, and wine buyers, though not necessarily sophisticated, had some sense.

There were other factors that were also considered but they were not significant. On balance, the TTAB found that there was no likelihood of confusion. The case took roughly four years to decide. Ms. Martelli represented herself and to her credit, she prevailed. But regardless of whether her winery racked up tens of thousands or hundreds of thousands of dollars in attorneys' fees, the proceeding must have taken precious time and attention away from her winery.

Lesson Learned: A logo trademark registration is not as powerful as a word mark (just words, no graphics) registration. So, after the case was decided, Bell's filed yet another federal trademark application in 2011 (on BELL'S, without any graphics) for beer, clothing and several other goods, and this version of the mark became registered in 2012.

Ravenswood vs. Black Raven Brewing

In the preceding Bell's Brewery v. Bell Hill TTAB opposition, beer was not sufficiently close to wine–given the marks in question. By contrast, consider the case of Franciscan Vineyards, owner of trademark registrations on RAVENS and RAVENSWOOD for wine. In this case, the TTAB found that BeauxKat Enterprises LLC's application for the mark BLACK RAVEN BREWING COMPANY for beer was confusingly similar to the RAVENS mark.

While the two logos in question look very different, as shown below, the trademark registrations and applications in this situation did not contain any logos so the TTAB compared the words only.

Ravenswood logo

Black Raven logo

The TTAB's analysis focused on the following:

First, how close are the two marks? The TTAB considered "RAVEN" in the words BLACK RAVEN BREWING COMPANY to be the "dominant" part of the mark. Why? Because ravens are all black and "brewing company" is a descriptive part of the mark. Accordingly, the dominant part of each mark (RAVEN and RAVENS) was essentially the same. Although RAVENS is plural and RAVEN is singular, the difference between singular words and plural words is usually of no or very little importance when analyzing whether there is a likelihood of confusion.

Second, how close are the goods? As in the Bell's Brewery case, the TTAB said that beer and wine are related because both are alcoholic beverages and both are often sold in the same stores and occasionally made by the same company.

Third, how strong is the first trademark? Although not famous, the RAVENS mark had some strength. RAVENS is unrelated to wine, and so is an "arbitrary mark" in relation to the goods. Arbitrary marks (and made-up words) are strong marks.

Fourth, are consumers sophisticated and/or is this type of good an "impulse" buy, or is it purchased after a lot of thought? As in the Bell's Brewery case, the TTAB concluded that wine was generally not an impulse buy, and wine buyers, though not necessarily sophisticated, had some sense.

The TTAB reached its conclusion that there was a likelihood of confusion after a couple of years. The result was that Black Raven Brewing Company could not register its name as a trademark for beer. However, Black Raven Brewing Company still operates the brewery using that mark. So why did Franciscan Vineyards fight to keep BLACK RAVEN BREWING COMPANY from being registered?

Registration of BLACK RAVEN BREWING COMPANY would have taken away from some of the strength of the RAVENS and RAVENSWOOD registrations had Franciscan Vineyards allowed it to be registered. Every new trademark registration that is close to an existing mark weakens the existing mark.

Lesson Learned: When selecting a trademark, do not ignore trademarks of other goods and services, especially those of related goods. Moreover, just because you have reached the conclusion that your mark is different enough from the rest to be okay to use and register does not mean a third party would agree with you. Consider whether the mark is close enough to another mark that the trademark owner may still come after you. Avoid this "gray zone" (where safety from infringement claims is iffy), unless you have a substantial risk tolerance and litigation budget to back it up.

CHAPTER 11

GOOD AND BAD PAIRINGS: HOW CLOSE MUST THE GOODS BE TO INFRINGE?

To find "trademark infringement," a court uses the "likelihood of confusion" test. The court must determine that potential purchasers of the goods or services with the allegedly infringing mark are likely to be confused as to source, origin or sponsorship of the goods or services. This test involves many factors. For example, in federal court in California[17] the test involves eight factors. In other areas of the country there may be more or fewer factors, but the tests are still roughly similar. In my experience, the most important factors, especially in trademark office proceedings, are normally:

1) How strong is the trademark owner's mark? (e.g., "Gallo" is very strong because of its extensive sales and marketing).

2) How close is the infringing mark in sound, appearance or other way to the trademark owner's mark?

3) How close are the infringing goods and services sold using the mark?

Five additional factors are:

4) Has there been actual confusion of potential purchasers?

5) Did the alleged infringer intend to trade on the goodwill of the trademark owner?

6) How close are the channels of trade (generally, do both

---

17 This test is the same in federal court in all states and territories within the jurisdiction of the United States Court of Appeals for the Ninth Circuit.

trademark owners sell their goods or services in the same way, e.g., by online, physical catalog or brick-and-mortar channels, and are they sold to individuals, retailers, distributors, wholesalers or other types of businesses)?

7) Are potential purchasers sophisticated and careful or are they unsophisticated and impulsive?

8) How likely is it to potential buyers that the trademark owner would expand into the same line of products or services as the alleged infringer?

This multifactor test may be applied differently depending upon the judge, jury or court of appeal in litigation, or an examining attorney or TTAB in Trademark Office proceedings. These variations in how the test is applied create much of the gray zone mentioned before (where it is not easy to tell whether or not there is infringement or whether or not a mark will get registered). For example, in *E. Remy Martin & Co., S.A. v. Shaw-Ross International Imports, Inc.*, 756 F.2d 1525 (11th Cir. 1985), Remy Martin, maker of cognac and brandy, sued Roger Myers and Shaw-Ross for using F. Remy for wine.

Remy Martin vs. Roger Myers and Shaw-Ross

Remy Martin held registered trademarks on REMY MARTIN for cognac since 1963, claiming use since 1884. It also held registered trademarks for ST. REMY and REMY for brandy since 1976 and 1981, respectively. In the late 1970s, Remy Martin began a multimillion-dollar advertising campaign that touted REMY as a nickname for REMY MARTIN cognac.

Meanwhile, Myers began importing sparkling wine with the label F. REMY way back in 1947, registering that mark for wine and champagne in the U.S. in 1957. In 1970, to resolve a dispute in France between the parties, Myers agreed with Remy Martin that in France Myers would use F. REMY, instead of "REMY" alone, on wine.

Myers stopped importing F. REMY into the U.S. in 1976. In 1977, Myers chose not to renew his U.S. trademark registration on F. REMY, and so it lapsed. However, in 1981, he began selling F. REMY in the U.S. again and refiled an application on F. REMY that year. As a result, Remy Martin sued Myers for trademark infringement. Remy Martin asked the Court for a preliminary injunction, i.e., a court order that Myers must stop using F. REMY early in the lawsuit, before any trial.

To get a preliminary injunction, Remy Martin had to show irreparable harm if Myers continued to sell wine under the name F. REMY. Remy Martin also had to show a substantial likelihood that they would ultimately win the case. The Trial Court refused to grant the injunction, noting that it did not think Remy Martin had shown a likelihood of success or irreparable harm so Remy Martin appealed.

The Court of Appeal found that cognac (and brandy) are distilled from wine, and therefore, are similar enough to wine that the public could easily conclude, seeing the F. REMY mark, that Remy Martin started to sell wine. Moreover, while there were some differences in the way the labels looked on the two products, the use of REMY alone by Remy Martin made the two marks (F. REMY and REMY) look very much alike. The two products were also sold in similar retail outlets (restaurants, bars and liquor stores) to the same type of customers.

Factors favoring Myers were that the Court found no "bad faith" and there was no evidence that anyone was actually confused.

The Appellate Court ruled in Remy Martin's favor. What carried the day for Remy Martin was that its rights in REMY had become quite strong as a result of its multimillion-dollar campaign, and Myers had abandoned his mark during the time of this campaign. The Appellate Court, therefore, reversed the Trial Court decision saying that Remy Martin should get the preliminary injunction.

Lesson Learned: If possible, avoid letting trademark registrations lapse. They can be very valuable. Because Myers let his initial U.S. trademark registration lapse and abandoned his use of F. REMY, his subsequent refiling of an application in 1981 did not have the benefit of his previous registration and use. Bear in mind that three years of nonuse of a trademark creates a presumption under federal law of abandonment (whether or not you have a federal registration). Had Myers continued some use and held onto his registration, there is little doubt that the case would have turned out differently.

E. & J. Gallo Winery vs. F. & P. S.p.A.

When the trademarks and the products being compared are close to each other (REMY for cognac and F. REMY for wine), it is relatively easy to understand a determination of infringement. But what happens when the products are less related, e.g., wine (or cheese) versus rice? While wine and cheese often go together, wine and rice or cheese and rice don't pair well.

In *E.&J. Gallo Winery v. F. & P. S.p.A.*, 899 F. Supp. 465 (E.D.Ca. 1994), Gallo noticed that F. & P. had managed to get a trademark registration on GALLO (as part of a logo) for rice. Gallo filed a petition to cancel F. & P.'s trademark registration in the Trademark Office. Subsequently, Gallo sued F. & P. in court for trademark infringement of its registered GALLO marks due to F. & P.'s use of GALLO for rice and other products.

While F. & P. litigated against Gallo for a while, ultimately their registration was canceled and they changed their trademark.

Lesson Learned: The *Gallo v. F. & P.* case tells us that the stronger the senior party's trademark, the further apart the goods can be while still holding the possibility of infringement. The moral of this story is, once again, to stay away from famous marks owned by powerful companies.

CHAPTER 12

WHEN GIANTS COLLIDE: TRADE DRESS AND LOGO PROTECTION

There are many names and varieties of wines, so it is sometimes difficult for a casual wine drinker to remember the name of a certain wine. Vintners and other business owners choose their logo with an eye for creating a lasting impression, knowing that a picture can make a much stronger impression than most words.

Most people hearing the term "trademark" think of words, but logos are protectable as trademarks too. Even images and "trade dress" can function as trademarks. Trade dress is simply the way packaging looks, such as that used for a bottle.

To be protectable, a logo or trade dress must have a certain uniqueness. A good rule of thumb to use on whether to register your logo or trade dress is to ask yourself: If a competitor started putting something that looks like my logo on its bottles, boxes or its website, would this bother me? If the answer is "yes," then consider registration.

Whether registered or not, a business has common law rights just by using a logo and/or trade dress. Just as in trademark law, if another mark so closely resembles yours that you feel it may cause a "likelihood of confusion" to the buyer, then it may be infringing.

How close is close? That depends on the likelihood of confusion factors, such as those mentioned in Chapter 11 about Remy Martin and Myers. When comparing trade dress or logos, it is important to consider how closely the other company's trade dress and/or logo compare to yours.

The case of *Kendall-Jackson Winery, Limited v. E. & J. Gallo Winery*, 150 F.3d 1042 (9th Cir. 1998) provides a good example of efforts to try to protect a logo and trade dress, and how it can be difficult to properly assess similarity of logos and trade dress.

Kendall-Jackson Winery vs. E. & J. Gallo Winery

Kendall-Jackson Winery (K-J) of Sonoma County, California, entered the wine market fast and furious. K-J was formed in 1983 and by 1994 was selling over $1,000,000 per year of its Vintner's Reserve premium wines. Also by that time, K-J's chardonnay was the number one seller in the U.S., with K-J's wines using a leaf logo.

Gallo Files the First Trademark Application

In 1995, E. & J. Gallo Winery entered the premium wine market with its Turning Leaf brand. Gallo also used a leaf logo, and the coloring of the leaf was somewhat similar to K-J's leaf. Gallo, knowing the importance of registration, filed a federal trademark application on its leaf logo in late 1995, which became a registration.

K-J Files the Second Trademark Application

After Gallo's 1995 trademark application, K-J filed an application on its leaf logo, which the U.S. Patent & Trademark Office (known affectionately as "the PTO" or "USPTO") granted. Even though K-J filed its application after Gallo, K-J was the first to use (the "senior user").

K-J Sues Gallo for Trademark and Trade Dress Infringement

K-J sued Gallo for trademark infringement. As previously noted, in many cases three of the likelihood of confusion factors are the most important: the similarity/dissimilarity of the marks, the strength/weakness of the senior user's mark and the similarity/dissimilarity of the goods or services. Here, the goods (wine) were obviously the same, and there was some general similarity of the logos in that they both use a leaf. However, K-J's use of a grape leaf for a logo was not very strong.

The Trial Court Finds No Infringement

On the claim of infringement of the grape leaf logo, the Trial Court found that a grape leaf was so pervasively used in the wine industry that this portion of the logo was not protectable. The Court also focused on the fact that Gallo's leaf logo did not look enough like K-J's leaf logo. The Court considered K-J's leaf logo's most distinctive part to be the words "Kendall-Jackson" passing through the leaf. Obviously, these words were not present in Gallo's leaf.

In addition, Gallo's leaf was rolled, not pointed down, and had different coloration. Therefore, the Trial Judge decided, without the need for a trial, that Gallo did not infringe K-J's leaf logo.

K-J also considered its trade dress to be unique and infringed by Gallo. On this issue of trade dress infringement there was a jury trial, because it was closer than the leaf logo issue. Nevertheless, the jury decided in favor of Gallo again.

The Appellate Court Affirms That There Is No Infringement

Then K-J appealed on both the logo and trade dress. The Appellate Court affirmed both decisions. On the logo issue, the Appellate Court found the broad idea of a grape vine leaf to be unprotectable on wine. The Appellate Court also found that Gallo's logo was sufficiently different from K-J's logo.

On the issue of trade dress, the Appellate Court upheld the jury's determination that K-J's trade dress was unprotectable. The Appellate Court described K-J's trade dress as bottles shaped in a "burgundy-style" or a "Bordeaux-style," having a rounded flange, a visible cork with printed leaves on it, a brown or burgundy neck label with gold lines on the top and bottom that form an oval in the back, and an off-white label featuring the multicolored leaf design.

Gallo's bottle was described in a similar manner. Current bottles used for K-J's Vintner's Reserve and Gallo's Turning Leaf are shown below to give a general idea of the trade dress.

K-J's bottle

Gallo's bottle

For trade dress protection, one must look at the trade dress as a whole, and determine if the combination of elements are unique and nonfunctional.

The labels on the K-J and Gallo wine bottles, above, look different. K-J's logo is crest-like, with the words "Kendall-Jackson" running through it. Gallo's logo separates the words from the leaf and does not have a crest-like appearance. The Court thought that K-J's logo jumped out more to the buyer than any impression of the overall look of K-J's bottle. Accordingly, the Court found that Gallo's trade dress was not confusingly similar to K-J's trade dress.

Lesson Learned: K-J did the right thing by registering its mark, although it should have done so sooner, but that is not why it lost. K-J overestimated the strength of its logo and bottle design. While K-J had extensive advertising and sales, helping to show a strong mark, the grape leaf portion of the logo was weak. Remember, the more common the image in your industry, the narrower the protection. The more unique, the stronger the protection. If you can, pick a unique image.

If the words, phrases, pictures, graphics or look of your product packaging is something you regard as unique, then protect it. Even if you have a federal registration on the words, consider protecting the words and the logo together and/or the logo alone. Each trademark–words alone, logo alone, and words plus logo–provides different protection which can be valuable. Also for logos, consider other protection, such as copyright. As for trade dress, it is not easy to get a trade dress registration. If you think the overall look of your bottle or packaging is unique, then consider protecting it.

CHAPTER 13

THE SQUEAKY TOY MAY NOT GET THE GREASE: PARODY IS RISKY

Many people find a good parody funny. However, when the parody is of your product, it may not be so funny. Jack Daniel's whiskey found itself in this situation as discussed in *VIP Products LLC v. Jack Daniel's Properties Inc.*, Case No. 14-2057 (D. Arizona, September 27, 2016).

The Jack Daniel's company is named after its founder, Jasper "Jack" Daniel. According to some accounts, he founded the Tennessee company in or about 1875 along with, oddly enough, a preacher and moonshine distiller named Dan Call. Mr. Call quit shortly thereafter, citing religious reasons.

In 1897, Jack Daniel's started using square-shaped bottles. According to accounts, the distillery was registered as No. 7 in the federal government's applicable district, but that number later changed. The original No. 7 inspired the "Old No. 7 Brand." The company boasts that it has sold over $10 billion of whiskey in the U.S. between 1997 and 2015.

VIP Products (VIP) made a dog toy that spoofed the venerable Jack Daniel's whiskey bottle. The toy, called "Bad Spaniels," is in the shape of a liquor bottle and has a picture of a wide-eyed cocker spaniel. The label says "Bad Spaniels" and "The Old No. 2, on your Tennessee Carpet." The label of a bottle of Jack says "Jack Daniel's Tennessee Sour Mash Whiskey" and "Old No. 7 Brand." Some of the words are in common. Also, "Bad Spaniels" rhymes with "Jack Daniel's." Yet, these words were different enough that, alone, there is no infringement.

VIP also copied the shape as well as the fonts and color scheme of the "Old No. 7 Brand" bottle. To help make sure consumers knew that the toy was not associated with Jack Daniel's, the packaging contained a disclaimer, namely: "This product is not affiliated with Jack Daniel's."

Jack Daniel's demanded that VIP stop selling the "Bad Spaniels" toy. The toy's square-shaped bottle, white lettering on black background, and font styles were all similar to Jack Daniel's. These and other similarities can be seen below:

Jack Daniels' bottle

VIP's bottle

Copying colors and font styles are not necessarily bad in themselves. Colors, alone, and font styles, alone, are hard to protect under trademark law. Generally, a company must sell a lot of product with a unique font style and/or unique color to get protection. Moreover, protection of the colors black and white is particularly difficult, because use of these colors is common place.

An example of a registered color is pink for insulation by Owens Corning. By contrast, the color black was not protected when used on an outboard motor (e.g., because black has a function that it goes with everything). Black was also not protected for a chocolate milk container.

An example of a protected font is the famous Coca-Cola® script mark. No one else in the beverage industry would likely get away with using the same font, especially if used in red. That script has been used for many years on countless Coke® bottles and cans as well as in many Super Bowl ads. The fonts used by Jack Daniel's are not as distinctive as the Coca-Cola® script.

With trade dress, each individual element or trademark need not be protected. There still can be protection in the aggregate. The more similarities that an alleged infringing product's packaging and/or labeling (the "Bad Spaniels" product) has in look to the packaging and labeling of a prior user (Jack Daniel's), the more chance of infringement.

One of VIP's defenses was that its product is a parody of a Jack Daniel's bottle. The "Bad Spaniels" toy does poke fun at Jack Daniel's whiskey. The juxtaposition of a dog's squeaky toy with hard liquor is funny. To be a successful parody, one must copy enough of the item being parodied to conjure up, in the viewer's mind, the product (i.e., Jack Daniel's).

However, there is no absolute right to parody. The test for trademark infringement is based on many factors. VIP's argument was that a parody (although not technically one of the factors) makes fun of the trademark and that is something that a trademark owner would not do to its own brand. Therefore, consumers should know VIP's dog toy is not sponsored or sold by Jack Daniel's.

One of the likelihood of confusion factors is "bad faith," e.g., the accused infringer's intent to capitalize on the goodwill of the trademark owner. So, there is a danger to VIP claiming that the "Bad Spaniels" toy is a parody. The danger is that VIP is admitting that it intended to copy and did copy enough of the Jack Daniel's bottle and label to conjure up the Jack Daniel's bottle in the squeaky toy buyers' minds. In any parody, the alleged infringer is capitalizing on the goodwill of the trademark owner.

VIP also claimed that Jack Daniel's trade dress is not protected because it is not distinctive and is functional. To that end, VIP asserted that there are several other companies using square liquor bottles.

Many elements of the Jack Daniel's bottle are not protected by themselves, such as the fonts and colors, and probably even the square-shaped bottle (taking as true VIP's assertion that a square liquor bottle is used by others to sell liquor). Nevertheless, the Court found that Jack Daniel's trade dress consists of the below:

> "a combination of a square bottle with a ribbed neck, a black cap, a black neck wrap closure with white printing bearing the OLD NO. 7 mark and a black front label with white printing and a filigreed border bearing the JACK DANIEL'S mark depicted in arched lettering at the top of the label, the OLD NO. 7 mark contained within a filigreed [fanciful or ornate] oval design in the middle portion of the label beneath the JACK DANIEL'S mark and the words "Tennessee Sour Mash Whiskey" in the lower portion of the label with the word "Tennessee" depicted in script."

The Court determined that the trade dress of the Jack Daniel's bottle, as described above, was not functional and was distinct, and therefore protectable. Note that in 2012, Jack Daniel's had obtained a trademark registration on its bottle with "Jack Daniel" written on the bottle's shoulder in two places (see below), but that registration was not infringed. As of early 2017, the case with VIP was still unresolved.

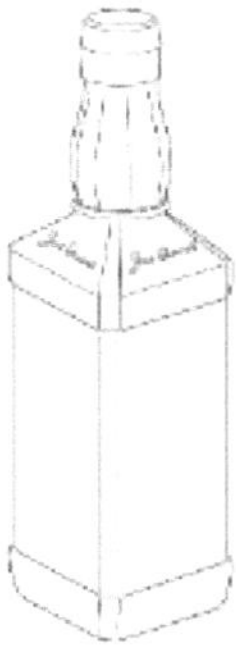

Lesson Learned: When seeking to copy elements of another's trademark or trade dress, consider whether these elements are unique in the aggregate. Trade dress can be tricky. The bottom line (except when dealing with famous marks) is whether a potential buyer will be confused as to sponsorship. Here, it is unlikely that a reasonable buyer would be confused. While well-known brands often expand into a variety of other product lines, the likelihood that Jack Daniel's would make a squeaky dog toy seems remote. Jack Daniel's asserts it sells many different products including clothing, bags, glasses, magnets, watches, posters and others, but none are close to dog toys.

Before copying elements of a competitor's trade dress such as fonts and colors, consider carefully whether buyers might associate the fonts and colors with the competitor, e.g., are the fonts and colors unique, how long has the competitor used them, and does the competitor sell a lot of product having these fonts and colors? In general, if you don't need to copy a font or color, there is no point in putting yourself in jeopardy of a lawsuit.

CHAPTER 14

HOW DO I LOOK? A UNIQUE BOTTLE DESIGN CAN BE PROTECTED

In the chapters on Kendall-Jackson versus Gallo, and Jack Daniel's versus VIP Products, trade dress was discussed as a type of protection for a unique bottle shape. Trade dress can not only include a unique bottle or package shape, but also the words, colors, fonts, and/or images on the bottle or package. Another type of protection available for a uniquely shaped product is called "design patent."

Lushious LLC of Yorktown Heights, New York, applied for a design patent on a wine bottle shaped somewhat like a women's leg in a high heel shoe, and the PTO issued Patent No. D703,543 on this unique bottle. What does this design patent mean for the competition?

In essence, a design patent means no one else can make, use, sell or offer for sale a product that, to the "ordinary observer," looks so similar to the patented design that the observer would think it is the patented product. Newly issued design patents have a 15-year term. After the term expires, the design is dedicated to the public, but there still may be trade dress protection.

One of the Coca-Cola Company's many trade dress registrations on bottles is shown here, US. Trademark Registration No. 2,155,915.

What is the difference between trade dress protection and a design patent? Trade dress protection requires that consumers recognize the shape of the bottle as indicating a particular source of the goods. In the case of Coke®, there is no doubt that almost all consumers recognize the shape as indicating Coke®. Also, trade dress protection can last for as long as one keeps selling the product.

In the case of the Lushious high heel shoe, if this wine bottle is not on sale or has only very limited sales, there would be no consumer recognition. A design patent protects the design regardless of consumer recognition. The downside is that a design patent only lasts a limited time.

Others in the wine industry have sought protection on unique bottles. The PTO issued a registration to Tosti SPA Corporation of Italy. This outline of a bottle with its "navel" (indentation) is covered by U.S. Trademark Registration No. 4,510,337 and owned by Tosti.

Tosti's Registration on bottle with navel

Tosti's actual bottle with navel

Another interesting bottle design (and trademark too) is the bottle for "ANOTHER!@#% MERLOT! (in a very cool bottle)" made by Bridgeview Vineyards, Inc. in Oregon. The bottle has an angled bottom, and leans like the leaning tower of Pisa.

It does not appear that Bridgeview registered this design, but Bridgeview does have a few registrations on trade dress, including U.S. Trademark Registration No. 2,393,703 as shown here. The trade dress is a bottle in the shape of a crescent moon having a human face.

Lesson Learned: Creating and using a unique product design can be expensive so protecting your investment in such a design makes a lot of sense. A unique product shape may be protected by trade dress or design patent–or both. Keep in mind that any design patent application is best done before the product is sold or otherwise made public. If there is (or you expect) consumer recognition of the product's packaging, trade dress protection may exist as well. As always, registration should be considered.

CHAPTER 15

THE WILD INTERNET FRONTIER: PROTECTING AGAINST DOMAIN NAME PIRACY AND OTHER PROBLEMS

Many business owners like to use their business name as a domain name. However, some businesses have instead opted to select a domain name that combines words that someone searching on the internet might use. For example, South Coast Winery Resort & Spa in Temecula, California, uses "wineresort.com" as a domain name, rather than its business name.

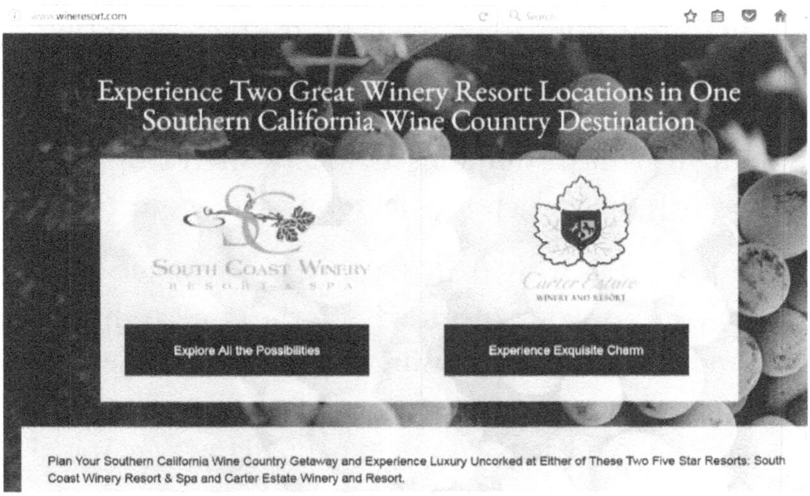

Printed by permission of South Coast Winery, Inc.

Suppose you prefer to use your company name, e.g.: "Smith and Jones Winery," but only want a portion of it–e.g. SmithAndJones.com–as the domain name. But when you try to register this domain name, you find someone else already owns the domain name and sells tires. The winery can't stop the tire company from using SmithAndJones.com unless Smith and Jones Winery is famous or there is trademark infringement. Most company names are not famous, so using that basis to stop the tire company normally won't work. In addition, tires are so unrelated to wine that typically there would be no trademark infringement in spite of the same or highly similar name.

Even if a company wants to use descriptive names as a domain name for its website, the company should also register its company name as a domain name, e.g., www.JuneauWinery.com, and then just forward to the main site at, e.g., www.bestwineryinAlaska.com. While one may be able to stop domain name piracy using trademark laws and/or anti-cybersquatting laws, proactive protection is less expensive.

Can using a domain name that is the same as or similar to a trademark of another company, cause a problem? Yes. When there is commercial use of a domain name, such as using the domain name as an address for a winery's or vineyard's website, then there is a potential for trademark infringement.

A rule of thumb is that if you select or have selected a domain name for your website that is the same as the business name, and if you have been using that business name for five or more years without a trademark issue, then you are probably relatively safe to use it as a domain name. However, it is always a good idea to do a trademark search before launching a site at that domain name, especially if the company has not had a site before.

An example of a cybersquatting case, which also illustrates the value of a famous mark, is *E. & J. Gallo Winery v. Spider Webs Ltd.*, 129 F. Supp. 1033 (S.D. Tex 2001), affirmed, 286 F.3d 270 (5th Cir. 2002). In this case, a company called Spider Webs Ltd. registered about 2,000 domain names, including

ErnestAndJulioGallo.com (the "E. & J. domain name"). Most of the 2,000 names were generic or descriptive and were offered for sale through Spider Web's internet site and on eBay. The E. & J. domain name was not offered for sale.

E. & J. Gallo ("Gallo") found out that Spider Webs owned the E. & J. domain name and so brought suit against Spider Webs to acquire the domain name. Since there was no website, at least initially, at the E. & J. domain name, there was no trademark infringement case. However, subsequently Spider Webs launched a site at the E. & J. domain name for commentary and discussions on the risks of alcohol use and alleged misrepresentation by corporations. The title of the site was "Spintopic."

To prove trademark infringement, Gallo would have to prove that customers, and/or potential customers, were confused as to whether or not Gallo owned or sponsored the "Spintopic" site due to the E. & J. domain name. Because it was unlikely that any reasonable person would think Gallo owned or sponsored this site, a claim of trademark infringement would be unlikely to succeed. That is where the fame of Gallo's mark comes in.

Federal antidilution law and some states' laws protect famous trademarks against commercial use even when there is no likelihood of confusion. To show trademark dilution, the following is required:

First, the plaintiff's mark is famous. Typically, but not always, this means that the plaintiff's mark is a household name.

Second, the defendant's mark or domain name is the same as or substantially similar to the plaintiff's mark. Variations, if any, generally must be relatively minor.

Third, the defendant's use of its "mark" is a commercial use or a use in commerce which dilutes the distinctiveness of the plaintiff's mark.

Since Gallo had several pending registrations, including ERNEST & JULIO GALLO, and since the registrations established a presumption of "distinctiveness," the Texas Court considered Gallo's mark to be protectable under Texas antidilution law.

The Court further found "dilution" because there was tarnishment of Gallo's brand (i.e., Spider Web's site was anti-alcohol and anti-corporation). Spider Web's use also reduced the distinctiveness and value of Gallo's mark. While Spider Webs had a disclaimer of any affiliation with the E. & J. Gallo company, that did not help in an antidilution claim.

The Court also found that Spider Webs violated the Anti-Cybersquatting Consumer Protection Act, 15 U.S.C. Section 1125. This Act allows a trademark owner to get a domain name from a person or company that registered that domain name, if the domain name registrant has a bad faith intent to profit from the domain name and registers, traffics in or uses a domain that is:

a) identical or confusingly similar to a distinctive mark,

b) identical or confusingly similar to or dilutive of a famous mark, or

c) is a trademark protected by 18 U.S.C. Section 706 (marks involving the Red Cross) or 36 U.S.C. Section 220506 (marks relating to the "Olympics").

The Court in the Gallo case had no trouble concluding that Spider Webs trafficked in domain names (having registered 2,000 of them), and that Spider Webs' business had nothing to do with "ErnestAndJulioGallo." The Court granted $25,000 in statutory damages to Gallo, which had sought the maximum of $100,000 per domain name.

Cybersquatting happens quite often, especially to famous brands. In 2009, Sutter Home had to bring an action to recover the domain name www.SutterHomeWines.com (*Sutter Home Winery Inc. v. Texas International Property Associates,* ICANN proceeding Claim No. FA0903001252751). That same year Mondavi also pursued a domain name squatter to get www.RobertMondaviWine.com (*Robert Mondavi Winery v. Top Business Names,* ICANN proceeding Claim No.: FA0906001270471).

Lesson Learned: The best way to prevent cybersquatting is to register the company name and its product names as trademarks, and register such names as domain names. Also, consider registering common company nicknames or abbreviations as trademarks and domain names, and common misspellings as domain names.

CHAPTER 16

SHH, IT'S A SECRET: KNOW AND PROTECT YOUR TRADE SECRETS

Some people are surprised to learn that there is a winery in every state, even Alaska. Possibly more surprising is that a bagel bakery in Ellsworth, Iowa became a $20 million-a-year business. How did it do that? The case of *Uncle B's Bakery, Inc. v Kevin O'Rourke and Brooklyn Bagel Boys, Inc.*, 920 F.Supp. 1405 (N.D. Iowa, 1996) explains.

Uncle B's Bakery vs. Brooklyn Bagel Boys

William Rose, Jr., spent some of his childhood in Chicago, where he grew to love bagels. When he went to the University of Iowa to study business, he longed for a good bagel. In 1985, not long after he graduated, he started Uncle B's Bagels in Ames, Iowa, and eventually opened a plant in Ellsworth.

Uncle B's sold bagels to grocery stores. At the time, the shelf life of bagels was anywhere from three to thirty days. Uncle B's created a process for extending the shelf life to well over three months for bagels kept in the refrigerated section. The process involved putting the bagels in an airtight plastic bag, then removing oxygen and putting carbon dioxide and nitrogen in its place. The company filed a patent application for this special preservation method.

After developing the special method, Uncle B's had a big competitive advantage in selling to grocery stores by guaranteeing a 90-day shelf life. According to court papers,

Uncle B's was careful to protect its trade secrets with the requirement that plant visitors had to sign a nondisclosure agreement (NDA).

About the beginning of 1994, when Uncle B's needed a plant manager, they interviewed Kevin O'Rourke. According to testimony, he signed Uncle B's NDA during his job interview so he could see the plant. Uncle B's then went on to hire O'Rourke. When both William Rose Jr. and his father welcomed O'Rourke aboard, they said they had him sign a more comprehensive employee NDA and a noncompete agreement. It was Uncle B's practice to have all employees sign an NDA and a noncompete agreement upon hiring. The signed agreements were kept in HR.

O'Rourke quickly became a trusted employee. He went to Europe with William Rose Jr. to help develop the bagel preservation process. However, within about a year, O'Rourke was hired by a competitor, Brooklyn Bagel Boys ("Bagel Boys") near Chicago. Fearing that O'Rourke would divulge their trade secrets, Uncle B's filed a lawsuit against the Bagel Boys and O'Rourke alleging several things, including misappropriation of trade secrets. Uncle B's also asked the Court for an injunction against O'Rourke working for the Bagel Boys.

It was clear that Uncle B's bagels were unique in that they were the only never-frozen bagels sold in refrigerated cases at supermarkets. But there was no evidence that Bagel Boys ever used any of Uncle B's secrets. There was only some evidence that the Bagel Boys started using a similar bag to Uncle B's, and O'Rourke said this bag was common in the industry.

The Court found that even if the bag was a stock material available from various packaging suppliers, there were still some trade secrets involved. For example, the specifications that the material must meet and the names of the actual suppliers were "secret" and protectable.

The Court also found that Uncle B's trade secrets were protectable even if used by Bagel Boys on products other than never-frozen refrigerated bagels, e.g., fresh bagels or frozen bagels. Moreover, the Court found that Uncle B's unique recipes, having special ingredients to prevent molding or staling, and its bagel-making processes were trade secrets.

Uncle B's had filed a patent application on its special preservation process. Could that process still be protected as a trade secret? The PTO had previously rejected the patent application, as it had considered the process obvious in view of prior patents and publications.

Even though the PTO had rejected the patent application, trade secret protection still existed because the process never became publicly known. The Court found the process eligible for protection because Uncle B's had invested seven years in development, the process was not in widespread use and it was not readily ascertainable by others.

Uncle B's also had to show that it took reasonable measures to protect its trade secrets. While Uncle B's could not produce O'Rourke's signed employee version NDA or the original noncompete agreement, both William Rose Jr. and Sr. said that they saw O'Rourke sign the agreements. Uncle B's also produced evidence that at least 148 out of 149 other employees had signed the employee version of the NDA and the noncompete agreements, and that O'Rourke had opportunities for unsupervised access to the HR office and files.

Generally, NDAs are enforceable. By contrast, a noncompete is often unenforceable against a former employee, depending on the state law being applied. For instance, in California, noncompete agreements are normally not enforceable against a former employee. In general, courts do not like to limit someone's right to earn a living.

While Uncle B's failed to secure its important HR documents against unauthorized access, there is little doubt that Uncle B's took several steps to protect its trade secrets. In addition, the Court appeared to have a healthy skepticism regarding O'Rourke's claim that he never saw or signed the NDA and noncompete.

So what does it take to prove you have a trade secret? Under the Uniform Trade Secrets Act, generally, the following:

A process, invention or other information that has economic value;

The information is "secret," i.e., not generally known in the industry, and is not readily ascertainable by others; and

The owner of the secret takes reasonable steps to maintain its secrecy.

Many businesses slip up on the last requirement by failing to take protective measures. Uncle B's did take such measures, such as making every plant visitor and every employee sign an NDA. So, even without a signed NDA and noncompete, and even before trial of the case on its merits, the Court enjoined O'Rourke from working at Bagel Boys, based on the Iowa Trade Secrets Act.

The first step in a good trade secrets' protection program is to devise a list of all of a company's trade secrets. For a winery or vineyard, these may include wine club member lists, vendor lists, customer lists, winemaking recipes and processes and grape growing processes, among others. Then, to protect these trade secrets, take the following steps:

1. Limit access to only those who need to know the secrets;
2. Use passwords for access to computers and computer files;
3. Have employees sign NDAs;
4. Lock doors and file cabinets; and
5. Give your attorney a copy of all NDAs and noncompete agreements upon execution.

Lesson Learned: Carefully review what information your company has which, if it fell into a competitor's hands and/or disappeared, would be a problem for you. Then make sure you take the right steps to protect it. Also, be sure to give your attorney a copy of any signed agreements, including nondisclosure and employment agreements, for safekeeping.

CHAPTER 17

TRADEMARK HIJACKING: WATCH OUT FOR INTERNATIONAL PIRATES

In 2016, wine exports from the U.S. were $1.62 billion. A growing portion of that wine goes to China, now the fifth-largest market for wine consumption behind the U.S., France, Italy and Germany.

Foreign markets can be a new revenue source for your business, but beware. When a trademark pirate registers your mark in its country, the true trademark owner may be unable to sell there under its own mark. Even worse, the trademark owner may get hit with a huge judgment as a result of a trademark infringement lawsuit brought by the pirate. This nightmare happened to one renowned French winemaker, Castel Freres SAS ("Castel").

The Case of Castel

Castel has been making wine since 1949, with its wines selling under that name worldwide. Castel first entered China in the late 1990s. It invested heavily there, including building a bottling plant. In 2001, Castel partnered with a Chinese company, Changyu wine.

Unknown to Castel, a Chinese company named Panati Wine (Shanghai) Co., Ltd. ("Panati") filed a trademark application in China on "KASITE," a Mandarin phonetic equivalent of "CASTEL." Since China is a "first to file" nation, the first filer of a trademark application has priority over a later filer. This priority means that even though Castel had been selling in China before Panati filed its application, Panati had superior rights to CASTEL.

Meanwhile, Castel was selling wine in China with the below label:

In 2003, Panati offered the trademark rights to Castel for one million Euros. Castel refused. It waited until 2005 and then opposed Panati's application, claiming Panati did not use the mark. However, Panati ultimately was able to prove use and won the opposition. Panati Wine (Shanghai) Co., Ltd. ("Panati") then sued Castel in China for trademark infringement demanding about $6 million.

After years of battling, Castel lost both its lawsuit and its appeal. Ultimately, Castel had to pay Panati about 34 million yuan (RMB) or about $5.5 million.

In May of 2014, China's new anti-trademark hijacking law took effect. This law might have saved Castel from its disaster. However, the anti-trademark hijacking law requires, among other things, that the true trademark owner oppose the trademark application of the hijacker. This puts the burden on trademark owners to keep a watch in China for trademark applications.

Lesson Learned: Whenever entering a foreign market, make sure to engage trademark counsel in that country to do a search and to file a trademark application on the company name and product names. In addition, if you are on the brink of becoming a famous brand, even if you are not exporting yet, consider registering in key foreign markets. Also consider monitoring foreign trademark applications (as well as monitoring in the U.S. if you aren't already).

CONCLUSION

TEN TIPS TO PROTECT YOUR INTELLECTUAL PROPERTY

In this book, I've outlined different scenarios where trademarks or copyrights were challenged or violated. In business, this sort of thing happens quite often–usually to those who least expect it. In providing this information, I hope that your business will recognize opportunities to better protect your brand so that you do not become the victim of an expensive and time-consuming lawsuit.

Here then, are ten tips that will put you on the right path to being more prepared when it comes to your valuable and unique product, company name or service.

1. CLEAR YOUR COMPANY NAME AND PRODUCT OR SERVICE NAMES

Whenever possible, before selecting a company, product, service or domain name, conduct a trademark clearance search. If you can, generate three to five possible names or marks. Don't let yourself get emotionally wedded to a mark at this stage. Then, trademark counsel will help you pick the safest mark to use. And remember, even if you would be willing to change your mark later in the event of a trademark snafu, rebranding and relabeling can be a huge headache and expense.

2. REGISTER YOUR COMPANY NAME AND YOUR PRODUCT AND SERVICE NAMES AS TRADEMARKS

Your company name should always be registered. A trademark registration enhances your ability to protect your name. Moreover, it acts as a "fence" for your intellectual property by clearly alerting others to your name and your intent to protect it.

Also, protect your product and service names, at least for products and services that are expected to sell well or are already selling well. Often, there is no substitute for the protection obtained by a federal registration.

3. BROADEN YOUR TRADEMARK RIGHTS

If you are selling or intend to sell goods and services beyond your core products or services, then consider filing trademark applications on your trademarks for those products or services. This broadens your rights, and can make enforcement much easier. Just because you have an existing trademark registration does not mean that it covers all of your important goods or services.

4. REGISTER YOUR COMPANY NAME AS A DOMAIN NAME

Your company name should be registered as a domain name. For example, if you own a winery named "A Midsummer Night's Dream," then register www.AMidsummerNightsDream.com. Also, consider registering common variations and misspellings, such as www.MidsummerNightsDream.com, www.MidsummerNight.com, etc.

5. PROTECT ANY UNIQUE PRODUCT PACKAGING OR PRODUCT DESIGN

If you have a unique product design, consider applying for a design patent. You should do so before you publicly display or use the product, publish images of the product, sell the product or offer the product for sale, and definitely not later than one year from the earliest date of these events. Also consider an application to register the unique product design or packaging as trade dress.

6. MONITOR AND ENFORCE YOUR TRADEMARKS

Proactively look for potential infringements of your trademarks. This is typically done by engaging trademark counsel to initiate a trademark watch. The earlier you find infringers in their sales, the easier it is to get them to change their name. Moreover, if you don't police your marks, your rights can become significantly eroded or even lost.

7. FILE COPYRIGHT APPLICATIONS

Any key artwork or graphics, and your website as a whole, are best protected against copying by a copyright registration.

8. MAKE SURE YOU OWN COPYRIGHT ON PHOTOS, ARTWORK AND TEXT

Make sure you own copyright for all of the photos and artwork used to market or promote your products and packaging. This includes any photos or graphics you use on your website. If the work was wholly created by your employee(s) acting within the scope of employment, then you own it.

However, if the work was created by a nonemployee (or an employee acting outside the scope of employment), unless there is a written assignment of copyright signed by the creator (author) of the work, you are not the owner. A "work made for hire" agreement will not normally transfer ownership of a work to you or your company for photos, graphics or text. Make sure to get a written and signed copyright assignment.

9. MAKE SURE YOU OWN YOUR INVENTIONS

Make sure that your employment agreements and your agreements with any independent contractors include an invention and trade secret assignment term, as well as a copyright assignment term.

10. PROTECT YOUR TRADE SECRETS AND CONFIDENTIAL BUSINESS INFORMATION

Important and simple steps to protect confidential information include:

a. Limit access by requiring passwords to gain access to a mailing list, customer list, purchase orders, proposals and financial information.

b. Limit access to any unique manufacturing or production information.

c. Ensure that your personnel with access to trade secrets and confidential business information acknowledge in writing that the company owns the trade secrets, including formulations, procedures, customer lists, financial information, mailing lists and any other confidential business information.

d. Have an acknowledgement of trade secrets and confidentiality requirements, as well as invention ownership terms, in your employment agreement or a separate agreement to be signed at the same time, i.e., when an employee is being hired. For already existing employees, have them sign these agreements, if you don't already have an agreement in place.

e. Enter into a nondisclosure or confidentiality agreement with anyone who may have or need access to your confidential information.

f. Give your attorney copies of all executed agreements, especially those that concern confidentiality, such as employment agreements and nondisclosure agreements.

For all of the above, it is best to consult with and obtain the assistance of qualified legal counsel.

APPENDIX

CHECKLIST AND INTELLECTUAL PROPERTY SELF-ASSESSMENT

1. Use the questions below to determine whether it is time to take some of the measures recommended in this book. Your answers will also better prepare you for a meeting with legal counsel who can then better evaluate your needs.
2. Would it trouble you if another business started using the same or a similar name as your business?
3. Would it trouble you if another business sold a product or service with a name, logo, graphics and/or look which is the same as or similar to that of your product or service?
4. Do you have a gift shop (physical and/or online) that sells goods with your business name on it?
5. Do you have artwork and/or photos on any of your product labels, website or marketing materials? If a competitor or third party copied text, artwork, photos, phrases or slogans from your website or marketing materials would it bother you?
6. Has anyone ever reviewed your website and marketing materials for potential infringement issues?
7. Do you have a customer list and/or mailing list? Would it bother you if a competitor had access to such lists?
8. Do you have a list of stores, retailers, distributors and/or other customers? Would it bother you if a competitor had access to it?
9. Do you have one or more processes, suppliers and/or parts/ingredients that your company developed that are

not generally known in the industry? Would it trouble you if a competitor found out this information and used it themselves?

10. Have you ever had a nonemployee create or provide artwork for marketing materials, your company website, product label or other use? Do you know if you own the copyright on the artwork? Do you know if you can make copies? Would it trouble you if a competitor used the same or similar artwork?

11. Do you know if you have any potentially patentable inventions (such as unique processes, formulations or devices)?

GLOSSARY

Alcohol and Tobacco Tax and Trade Bureau (**TTB**) is an office of the United States Department of the Treasury. It was originally the **Bureau of Alcohol, Tobacco and Firearms** (**BATF** or **ATF**) and became the **TTB** in 2003.

Appellation is the name of the geographic area or viticultural region where specific grapes are grown.

Certification of Label Approval (**COLA**) is a certification issued by the TTB to evidence that an alcoholic product is properly labelled in accordance with federal laws and regulations. A COLA is required in order to sell an alcoholic product.

Common law trademark rights are legal rights that a trademark owner obtains to exclude other companies from using a confusingly similar mark merely by virtue of using the trademark (selling product with the mark on it). Common law rights cover the geographic area in which the mark is used.

Intent-to-use (**ITU**) trademark application is generally one where the trademark owner (applicant) has not yet "used" the mark (or is not sure), but does have a "good faith" intent to use the mark.

Official Gazette (**OG**) is a periodic publication of the U.S. Patent & Trademark Office. Among other things, it contains trademark applications being published to see if any third parties want to oppose the application.

Summary judgment is when a court decides a lawsuit without having a trial. A litigant can request (make a motion for) summary judgment when it thinks there are only legal issues, and no dispute about any important facts. If the court agrees, it will grant the motion for summary judgment and thus decide the case.

Trademark Office usually is used to refer to the portion of the U.S. Patent & Trademark Office (**USPTO** or **PTO**) that handles trademark applications and registrations.

Trademark Trial and Appeal Board (TTAB) is the U.S. Patent & Trademark Office's tribunal that decides trademark opposition and cancellation proceedings, among other things.

Use in a trademark sense comes from actual sales of the goods with the trademark on the goods or their packaging, or actual sales of the services with the trademark used in advertisements for the services.

Viticultural region or area is a designated wine grape–growing area. Viticultural regions in the United States have boundaries defined by regulations of the Alcohol and Tobacco Tax and Trade Bureau (TTB).

Made in United States
Cleveland, OH
18 October 2026

46422855R20058